TRACING YOUR MEDICAL ANCESTORS

A Guide for Family Historians

MICHELLE HIGGS

Pen & Sword
FAMILY HISTORY

First published in Great Britain in 2011 by
PEN AND SWORD FAMILY HISTORY
an imprint of
Pen & Sword Books Ltd
47 Church Street
Barnsley
South Yorkshire
S70 2AS

ISBN 978 1 84884 277 9

A CIP catalogue record for this book is
available from the British Library

Typeset in 10pt Palatino by Mac Style, Beverley, East Yorkshire
Printed and bound in the UK by CPI

Pen & Sword Books Ltd incorporates the Imprints of Pen & Sword
Aviation, Pen & Sword Maritime, Pen & Sword Military,
Wharncliffe Local History, Pen and Sword Select, Pen and Sword
Military Classics, Leo Cooper, Remember When, Seaforth Publishing
and Frontline Publishing.

For a complete list of Pen & Sword titles please contact
PEN & SWORD BOOKS LIMITED
47 Church Street, Barnsley, South Yorkshire, S70 2AS, England
E-mail: enquiries@pen-and-sword.co.uk
Website: www.pen-and-sword.co.uk

CONTENTS

ACKNOWLEDGEMENTS

While writing this book, I received help and advice in locating information and illustrations from a number of different sources. I would like to express my gratitude to the following:

The staff of Birmingham Archives and Heritage Service; the School of Dentistry in Birmingham; Dudley Archives and Local History Service; the Wellcome Library, London; Dr Ian Paterson of the Northern General Hospital in Sheffield; and Robert Woods of Familyrelatives.com.

Special thanks are due to Peter Basham of the Royal College of Physicians of London, Fiona Bourne of the Royal College of Nursing Archives, Matthew Bradby of the Queen's Nursing Institute, Tim Crumplin of Clarks Archives, Howard Doble of London Metropolitan Archives, Neil Handley of the British Optical Association Museum, Dr Chris Hilton of the Wellcome Library, Briony Hudson of the Royal Pharmaceutical Society of Great Britain, Melanie Parker of the British Dental Association Museum, Frances Pattman of King's College London Archives and Andrea Peace of the Chartered Society of Physiotherapy.

I would also like to thank the following people who were so generous with their time and their research:

Nick Baker, Stephen Due, Clayton Ford, Gloria Hargreave, Paul Morrell, David Waddy and Richard Waddy.

Finally, I would like to thank my husband Carl for his patience and support, and my family and friends for their encouragement during the writing of this book.

INTRODUCTION

If you have a doctor, nurse or other medical professional in your family tree, there is a good chance you can find out more about his or her career from the available records. The likelihood of finding your ancestor listed depends to a large extent on when he or she lived and worked; for instance, for physicians, surgeons and apothecaries, there are more sources to try from the early nineteenth century onwards, while for nurses, the number of official records increases from the 1920s. The efforts of the various medical professions to organise themselves helped to enhance their status, and also created an invaluable paper trail for family historians.

Even if you cannot find your ancestor listed in any of the relevant sources, it is still possible to get a clearer picture of his or her working life from records of hospitals and professional associations, or from artefacts and photographs in medical museums.

This book aims to give an overview of the role, training and places of work for each medical professional included, as well as the sources which can be used to trace them. These include printed records, original sources and online databases. While online sources can give you a head start in your research, they are no substitute for visiting a specialist library or archive yourself.

It has not been possible to include every specialism or ancillary occupation, and this book is in no way intended to be a definitive history of the medical profession. A bibliography is therefore included in the appendices where you will find listings of more detailed publications about specific medical professions. Also in the appendices is a useful contacts section, with listings of relevant archives, museums and professional associations, in addition to a glossary of medical qualifications, and lists of the various terms and titles used to describe nurses.

How to use this book

This book is broadly split into four sections: the medical profession, the nursing profession, patients and sources. Within these sections, the professions are split out further with background information on working conditions, training and qualifications. In the places of work chapters, you will find more specific information about the areas in which your ancestor could have worked – for example, hospitals, the British Army or general practice. There is also a development of the profession section, which deals with various specialisms in both the medical and nursing professions, such as gynaecology, radiography and district nursing.

Throughout the book, you will find case studies of real people whose careers have been traced using the available records. The sources section discusses these records and others in greater detail, showing how they can be used to trace your medical ancestor. This book assumes you have no previous knowledge of family history, but if you already know the basics of genealogical research, simply dip into the sections you are most interested in.

Section 1
THE MEDICAL PROFESSION

Chapter 1

THE ROLE OF THE MEDICAL PROFESSION

Before the nineteenth century, qualified medical men were divided into three distinct categories: physicians, surgeons and apothecaries. Physicians were without question at the top of the tree in terms of status. They were the rarest of the medical profession, having a university degree (although not always in a medical subject), and they alone held the qualification MD (Doctor of Medicine) and the title of 'doctor'. They attended patients to offer advice and suggest remedies for ailments, charging high fees for the privilege. They did not dispense any medication and tended to practise only in the larger towns and cities where there was a suitably wealthy clientele.

In the eighteenth century, physicians could study at Oxford, Cambridge, Edinburgh, Glasgow, Aberdeen or St Andrews universities to obtain their degrees. Would-be physicians who were non-Anglicans were excluded from British universities, and instead studied abroad, with Leiden, Rheims and Padua being the most popular. At this time, physicians were the only members of the medical profession to be accepted in society as gentlemen.

Originally known as barber-surgeons, surgeons qualified through a practical apprenticeship rather than an academic education. Although barbers in London had been linked with surgeons since the thirteenth century, it was not until 1540 that an Act of Parliament united the Barbers' Company and Fellowship of Surgeons as the Barber-Surgeons' Company of London.

Surgeons were not allowed to provide internal medicines of any kind. Their work was manual, and it ranged from carrying out amputations, lancing boils and treating syphilitic sores, through to pulling teeth and blood-letting. The occupation of surgery was therefore seen as menial, though its prestige increased considerably when the Company of Surgeons split from the barbers in 1745. The surgeons sought professional recognition as the rise of private anatomy schools and the beginnings of an academic basis for surgical practice further increased their status. By 1800, the Company of Surgeons was granted a royal charter to become the Royal College of Surgeons in London (later England).

From the early sixteenth century, both physicians and surgeons had to be licensed to practise their professions. Under a statute of 1512, issued by Henry VIII, they could apply for medical licences from the bishops of England and Wales. Under this statute, they were not allowed to practise unless they had been examined by medical practitioners and received a licence from the diocesan bishop.

Physicians could also be licensed by the Royal College of Physicians of London, as long as they held a medical degree. The Royal College was founded in 1518, and in the early years College licences were held mainly by those practising in London. This was despite the fact that an Act of Parliament in 1523 extended the College's licensing powers to the whole of England, not just London. Those who held College licences did not need to be licensed by a bishop as well. This system of ecclesiastical licensing (which also included midwives) died out in the mid-eighteenth century.

Apothecaries also trained through an apprenticeship, dispensing and selling medicines, usually from a shop. They could charge fees for the drugs they provided, but not for their advice. While the whole medical profession was run on a business basis, this was perhaps more evident for apothecaries as their work involved retailing to the public.

From the early nineteenth century, increasing numbers of apothecaries, both in London and the provinces, were undertaking work which could be called 'general practice'. They sought recognition of this from the rest of the medical profession, pushing for reform that would allow them to charge fees for attending patients, instead of surcharging on the medicines they dispensed. The result was the Apothecaries Act of 1815 which, among other things, recognised the Society of Apothecaries as a medical licensing body.

In Scotland, the situation was different. David Hamilton explains in *The Healers* that 'the surgeon-apothecary was well established as a general practitioner, and hence apothecaries did not exist in Scotland. Their role was taken over by the new dispensing chemists.'

Although surgeons and apothecaries continued to practise as specialists in their field, the title of 'surgeon-apothecary' became more common as the skills of both occupations were combined into one. As Joan Lane points out in *A Social History of Medicine*, surgeon-apothecaries were the 'equivalent of the modern general practitioner'.

Apprenticeships were the standard way of gaining qualified status in most trades in Britain before the nineteenth century. In fact, it was illegal to practise a trade without being apprenticed or qualified. From the age of 14, a boy was apprenticed to a qualified master, usually for a term of seven years. The boy lived in his master's house and undertook his apprenticeship without pay. His parents, or guardians of the parish if he had no family, paid the master a premium in a lump sum, which would cover tuition, board and lodging during the whole term of the indenture. If a son was apprenticed to his father, no premium was paid.

It was the premium that determined which occupation a boy could follow, as it had to be affordable for his parents or guardians. Since premiums were high for apprentice surgeons and apothecaries, this automatically limited the class of boy who could aspire to enter these professions. By the early nineteenth century, premiums had risen considerably because the medical profession itself had increased in social status, and it was known there were good profits to be made from a successful medical practice.

The terms of medical apprenticeships varied between five and seven years. Special requirements of the medical apprentice included being literate and numerate, as well as having a rudimentary knowledge of Latin. Although apprenticeships could be arranged through family connections or other personal contacts, by the 1750s – when the medical profession was expanding – it was common for medical apprenticeships to be advertised in local newspapers. The master was not usually named, nor was the cost of the premium mentioned. Instead, interested parties were directed to send references or make contact with a 'middle man', such as a chemist, medical-instrument maker or the newspaper itself.

Many advertisements stressed the need for prospective apprentices to have a classical education, to come from a respectable family and to be around 15 or 16 years old. As the advertisements were aimed at the apprentice's parents, who were to pay the premium, the majority stated that he would be treated like one of the family. Hospitals could also advertise apprenticeships from time to time.

In 1821, the following advertisement appeared in the 5 March issue of the *Morning Chronicle*:

VACANCY for a MEDICAL APPRENTICE – A Gentleman in the vicinity of the great Medical Schools of the West end has a VACANCY for an ARTICLED STUDENT, whose studies will be combined with Hospital practice, and attendance upon Lectures during the greater part of the Apprenticeship. The Plan of Instruction embraces the visiting of and prescribing for Patients, and frequent Examinations in

Morbid Anatomy &c. Particulars at Mr Weiss's, surgeons-instrument maker, 62, Strand.

Many advertisements stressed the wide range of experience that the apprentice could glean from the apprenticeship, particularly when the master was attached to a hospital or other public institution, which often meant a workhouse. The *Ipswich Journal* ran this advertisement in their issue dated 30 July 1825:

MEDICAL APPRENTICE. A Gentleman established in the Practice of Physic and Surgery, for the last 25 Years in the Neighbourhood of the large Hospitals in London, has a VACANCY for an Apprentice. There is attached to the Practice, a very large Public Institution, and a large district of Out-door Poor, giving on average from 40 to 50 patients daily for the attention of the Pupil – thus affording opportunities for instruction and improvement in an eminent degree. Twelve Months attendance on the Midwifery Practice of the Institution, which is very extensive, will be allowed at the expiration of the term of Apprenticeship. For particulars, apply (Post Paid) to Mr Edward Revans, Yoxford.

The cost of the premium depended on the reputation of the master and where he lived. For instance, if he was a well-established surgeon living in London or one of the provincial cities or spas, he could justifiably charge far higher fees than someone with a modest practice in a small market town. Premiums were also higher in the provinces if the master was an honorary surgeon at one of the new hospitals, rather than just being in private practice. The custom of medical apprenticeships started to die out in the 1860s.

A minority of young men who had completed their medical apprenticeships took extra courses provided in hospitals by honorary consultants. This work gave them greater experience of a wider range of cases, and brought them into contact with eminent practitioners who might become their patron if sufficiently impressed by their skill and aptitude. There was a certain kudos attached to studying with the leading consultants and if a medical man could prove he had taken lectures with experts in their field, particularly in London, this would stand him in good stead if he applied for a position as a resident surgeon or physician at another hospital. These posts were also known as house surgeons, house physicians or junior housemen.

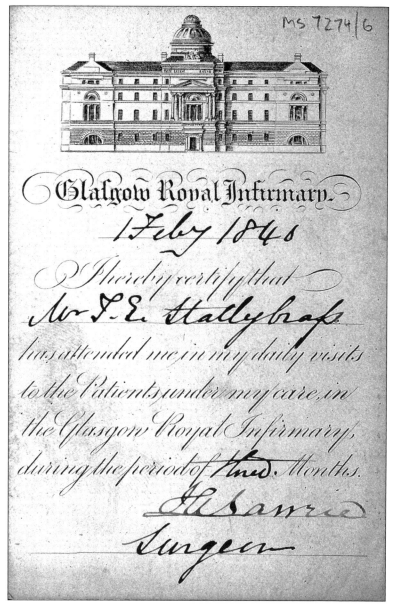

Certificate confirming that T E Stallybrass attended J A Lawrie, surgeon, during his daily visits to patients at Glasgow Royal Infirmary, 1848. (Courtesy of the Wellcome Library, London)

In 1834, the Select Committee on Medical Education heard that in London there were two distinct ways of gaining extra experience, both of which involved additional expense for the student or his parents. If he could afford it, the best experience was to be gained as a 'dresser' for twelve months, which in 1834 cost around £500. Less well-off students could become 'pupils' of a particular consultant, walking the wards with him. This cost £26 5s for a year's tuition. Lecture fees were extra, as were courses in physiology and *materia medica*, examination fees, books and specimens for dissection.

THE WAINWRIGHTS, SURGEONS OF DUDLEY, WORCESTERSHIRE

The sons of physicians, surgeons and apothecaries often followed in their fathers' footsteps, so it is not unusual to find two, three or even four generations of medical professionals in the same family. The Wainwrights of Dudley typify this tradition, being surgeons in the town in the eighteenth and early nineteenth centuries. Their apprenticeships are all recorded in the source *Eighteenth Century Medics* by P J and R V Wallis (see the sources section).

Born in 1700, Thomas Wainwright was the first to follow a career in surgery; his father Philip had been a nail-maker. In Philip's will, dated 1712, he left £1 to pay for Thomas's education for five years after his death. *Eighteenth Century Medics* records that in 1715, Thomas of Sedgley, Staffordshire, was apprenticed to Bernard Perkes, barber-surgeon. His widowed mother Anne signed the apprenticeship papers. Almost thirty years later in 1744, Thomas is recorded as being a master himself, taking on Joseph Slaney as an apprentice for five years at a premium of £52. It is likely that he had other apprentices during the intervening years who were not recorded.

Although Thomas married in 1722, it was not until 1741 that his only surviving son, Joseph, was born. Joseph became a surgeon himself and it is probable that he was apprenticed to his own father, for which no premium would have been paid. *Eighteenth Century Medics* records that in 1774, Joseph took an apprentice, Thomas Crane, for five years at a premium of £70 – but this was not necessarily his first apprentice. In 1784, 1790 and 1791, three more apprentices followed, all for seven years at an

Eighteenth-century surgeon John Hunter, FRS, from the picture by Joshua Reynolds. (Illustrated London News, 14 October 1893)

increased premium of £105. The source also notes that Thomas Wainwright was subscribing to medical books between 1755 and 1801, so we can estimate that he was a practising surgeon from 1755 onwards.

From 1796, Joseph and Thomas are recorded as taking on apprentices together, so they were working as a partnership from this time. However, this was Thomas Junior, the son of Joseph (born in 1770), not Thomas Senior, Joseph's father.

As the Wainwrights were practising surgeons in the eighteenth and early nineteenth centuries, they cannot be found in the *Medical Directory* or *Medical Register*, which started in 1845 and 1859 respectively. However, there are entries in the earlier, non-compulsory *Medical Register* for 1779, 1780 and 1783. This eighteenth-century *Medical Register* was issued on commercial lines, unlike the later, completely separate, Victorian *Medical Register*, which was produced by the General Medical Council and set up to regulate the medical profession. In 1779, 'Mr Joseph Wainwright' is recorded as a surgeon in Dudley, and the entry is the same for the following year and 1783.

They are also listed in the early trade directories for Worcestershire. In 1780, Joseph Wainwright is recorded as a surgeon in High Street, Dudley, while *Holden's Triennial Directory* for 1809–11 lists 'Wainwright Joseph and Son, Surgeons, High Street, Dudley'. By 1820, *Lewis's Worcestershire Directory* lists 'Wainwright & Roberts, Surgeons of High Street, Dudley', so Joseph Wainwright had probably died between the publication of the directories.

In *Pigot & Cos. Directory* for 1828–29, which covers Worcestershire, John Roberts is listed as a surgeon in High Street, Dudley but there are no Wainwrights. This is probably because Thomas Wainwright is listed as a 'gentleman' in the 'Nobility, Gentry and Clergy' section.

Thomas Wainwright was an astute businessman and may have been the same man who was mayor of Dudley for 1820. His name is mentioned in countless documents relating to land transactions held at Dudley Archives and Local History Service.

Chapter 2

TRAINING AND QUALIFICATIONS

New legislation

In the nineteenth century, those who could not afford the services of qualified medical men had plenty of unqualified medical practitioners to choose from. These included 'bone-setters' (people who set broken or dislocated bones), 'leechmen', water casters (who judged diseases by analysing urine) and aurists (ear specialists), along with the 'local woman' who was regularly used as an assistant during childbirth and as an abortionist.

The growth of the medical profession and its rise in status meant that new standards were required to differentiate and distance the professionals from unqualified practitioners. This began with the foundation of the Royal College of Surgeons in 1800 and with the passing of the Apothecaries Act in 1815. After the Royal College was founded, those who became members could take an examination leading to the qualification MRCS (Member of the Royal College of Surgeons).

Standards were also raised for apothecaries and the 1815 legislation stipulated that they had to be licensed by the Society of Apothecaries in order to practise, obtaining the qualification LSA (Licentiate of the Society of Apothecaries). To become licentiates, they had to pass examinations and attend lectures on anatomy, chemistry, botany, *materia medica* and the theory and practice of physics, proving their attendance through certificates signed by their lecturers.

A further requirement was to undertake a six-month placement, working in a hospital, infirmary or dispensary, though this did not have to be full time or in a single block. It was common for students to spend a year or more of their apprenticeship in London attending lectures and undertaking clinical training.

The LSA and the MRCS became the most popular qualifications for medical professionals. As Steven Cherry notes in *Medical Services and the Hospitals in Britain 1860–1939*, by the 1840s almost 95 per cent of newly qualified medical professionals were members of the Royal College of Surgeons and licentiates of the Society of Apothecaries. They were to be the new surgeon-apothecaries.

In 1843, the Royal College of Surgeons nominated 600 fellows from its members, and in the following year a higher qualification was introduced: the FRCS (Fellow of the Royal College of Surgeons). From this date, it was necessary to hold the FRCS before entering surgical training and going on to specialise in surgery. By 1854, there were approximately 200 fellows and 8,000 members of the Royal College of Surgeons. At this time, most of their operations were performed at their patients' homes.

Despite these developments in raising standards for apothecaries and surgeons, as late as 1834, a man could become a member of the Royal College of Physicians by taking three twenty-minute examinations and paying the sum of 50 guineas. According to Sir David Barry, who gave evidence to the Select Committee on Medical Education in that year, anyone could pass the examination 'who is a good classical scholar but knows nothing of chemistry, nothing of medical jurisprudence, nothing of surgery, little or nothing of anatomy, nothing of the diseases of women in childbed, and nothing of the manner of delivering them'.

The Medical Act of 1858

It was not until 1858 that the landmark Medical Act was passed, which required medical professionals to be licensed by one of nineteen licensing bodies. A year later, the *Medical Register*, in which all qualified medical professionals had to appear in order to practise medicine, was established. The Act also set up the General Medical Council to oversee all aspects of licensing and education.

The new legislation, however, missed the opportunity to establish a single basic qualification in medicine, surgery and midwifery, so numerous qualifications continued to be used. The Act also did not outlaw unlicensed practitioners so 'quacks' continued to dispense their services, either in person or by post.

There were nineteen different medical licensing bodies in the UK at that time, and representatives from each one sat on the General Medical Council. They included the following (listed in the order in which they appear in the *Medical Register*):

Royal College of Physicians of London
Royal College of Surgeons of England
Apothecaries' Society of London

University of Oxford
University of Cambridge
University of Durham
University of London
Royal College of Physicians of Edinburgh
Royal College of Surgeons of Edinburgh
Faculty of Physicians and Surgeons of Glasgow
University of Edinburgh
University of Aberdeen
University of Glasgow
University of St Andrews
King and Queen's College of Physicians in Ireland
Royal College of Surgeons in Ireland
Apothecaries' Hall of Ireland
University of Dublin
Queen's University in Ireland

In 1883, the Royal University of Ireland joined the list, followed three years later by the Victoria University of Manchester. Other universities were added over the years, including Birmingham (1900), Liverpool and Leeds (1904), Sheffield (1905), Bristol (1910) and the University of Wales (1912). Medical students had previously been able to take courses at medical schools in these provincial centres, but they had not been able to take their medical degrees there. In 1907, the Royal University of Ireland was dissolved, becoming the National University of Ireland. The Queen's University of Belfast became a licensing body in 1910.

In 1860, the Royal College of Physicians of London instituted the membership examination (MRCP) as the qualification for physicians. The MRCP replaced the licence (LRCP), which itself was remodelled into a complete qualification through the addition of surgery and midwifery to its requirements.

The Medical Act 1886 Amendment Bill

In 1886, new legislation was passed to revise the original Medical Act, more than thirty years after it had been entered on the statute books. The Medical Act 1886 Amendment Bill made it compulsory for all qualified medical professionals to be examined in medicine, surgery and midwifery.

ANDREW CLARK, PHYSICIAN

Many newly qualified medical professionals chose to specialise as physicians or surgeons. Andrew Clark (later Sir) did just that, rising to become president of the Royal College of Physicians of London later in his career. He was born in Aberdeen in 1826, the only child of a surgeon, but he was orphaned at an early age and was brought up by two uncles.

Andrew Clark's obituary in the *Lancet* reveals that he began his medical apprenticeship at the age of 13 in a druggist's shop in Dundee. The *British Medical Journal*, however, states that he served a four-year apprenticeship with Dr Alexander Wilson, a Dundee surgeon. This indicates the discrepancies which can sometimes be found in newspaper reports. The *Medical Register* records that he gained his degree at Marischall College at the University of Aberdeen in 1854 and became a fellow of the Royal College of Physicians four years later.

Sir Andrew Clark, physician. (The Strand Magazine, 1893)

However, his obituaries in both the *Lancet* and the *British Medical Journal* point out he also had a military career, which is not mentioned in the *Medical Register*, underlining the value of such additional information sources. This information is backed up by his entry in the *Lives of the Fellows of the Royal College of Physicians of London* (otherwise known as *Munk's Roll*).

While an apprentice, Andrew Clark studied at the Tay Square Academy and attended the wards of the Royal Infirmary. He studied in Edinburgh as an extra-academical student in 1842 and from 1843 to 1846, and developed an early interest in pathology, becoming an assistant in the pathological department of the Royal Infirmary. He took the English

MRCS diploma in 1844, but this is not referred to in the *Medical Register* or *Medical Directory*.

Still unqualified at the age of 22, Andrew Clark started experiencing symptoms of tuberculosis, and in 1846, he joined the navy as an assistant surgeon 'so that he might obtain the benefits of an out-door life'. He stayed for seven years, and for much of that time he was involved in pathological work at Haslar Hospital.

In 1853, when the post of conservator of the pathological museum of the London Hospital became available, Andrew Clark left the navy and was successfully appointed. A year later, he gained his MD from Aberdeen and was elected as assistant physician to the London.

Alongside his hospital work, Andrew Clark built up a successful private practice in Montague Street, Bloomsbury, and became full physician to the London in 1866. He was made consulting physician there twenty years later, a post he also held at the City of London Hospital for Diseases of the Chest, as well as at the East London Hospital for Children. Andrew Clark was made a baronet in 1883 and was elected president of the Royal College of Physicians five years later, retaining his post until his death in 1893.

CHRISTOPHER MARTIN, SURGEON

Not all successful medical professionals in the Victorian period came from rich families. Christopher Martin was born in 1866 in Stockton-on-Tees, the son of a wharfinger. According to his entry in *Lives of the Fellows of the Royal College of Surgeons* by Sir D'Arcy Power and W R Le Fanu, he was educated at a Society of Friends' school and then at Middlesbrough High School. From there, he studied medicine at Edinburgh University, graduating with first-class honours MB (Bachelor of Medicine) and CM (Master of Surgery) in 1887.

In the Wellcome Library, there is a press cutting from a Middlesbrough newspaper that refers to Christopher Martin. Dated 3 December 1887, with the heading 'A Successful Middlesbrough Student', the short report details his success at Edinburgh and also states that he was the son of Mrs Martin, the matron of the North Riding Infirmary. It notes that he

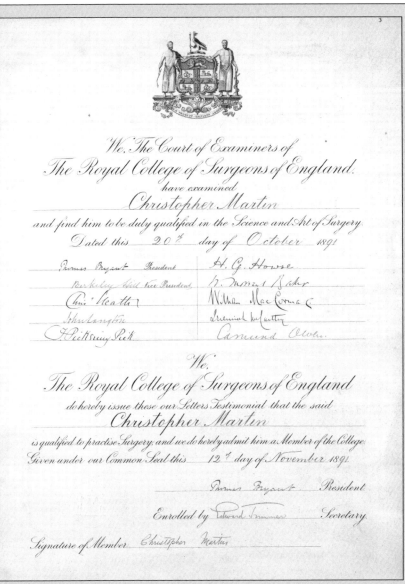

Medical qualification certificate awarded to Christopher Martin by the Royal College of Surgeons, 1891. (Courtesy of the Wellcome Library, London)

won three first medals at the university in senior surgery, midwifery and physiology, and a first medal in practical anatomy at the College of Surgeons. This success led him to be appointed demonstrator of anatomy and practical physiology while he was a student. The report continued: 'He was also awarded the "Scott Scholarship" for being the best man of the year 1887 in midwifery and diseases of women, and the Beaney Prize for being the best man of the year in surgery, anatomy and physiology, but was debarred from holding them because he was under age.' This is a reference to the fact that he did not turn 21 until late in 1887.

Christopher Martin's entry in the *Medical Register* records that he gained an MB and Master of Surgery in 1887 from the University of Edinburgh and became a fellow of the Royal College of Surgeons of England in 1891. He was also a fellow of the Royal College of Obstetricians and Gynaecologists.

His early interest in midwifery and diseases of women was to shape the rest of his medical career. According to Sir John Peel's *Lives of the Fellows of the Royal College of Obstetricians and Gynaecologists 1929–1969*, Christopher Martin spent some of his post-graduate education at St Bartholomew's Hospital in London, where he met Lawson Tait, the eminent abdominal surgeon. He invited Christopher to be his assistant in Birmingham, and in 1890 Christopher was appointed as assistant surgeon to the Midland and Birmingham Hospital for Women. Later, he was appointed as assistant to the professor of gynaecology at Queen's College, Birmingham.

Christopher Martin was associated with the Midland and Birmingham Hospital for Women for the rest of his life. He subsequently became surgeon to the institution, and was made consulting surgeon in 1920. He was instrumental in helping to found a new hospital in 1904. Peel's *Lives* records that he was 'amongst the first to use radium in the treatment of cancer of the cervix, and did much to popularise abdominal hysterectomy'. During the First World War, Christopher Martin served at the First Southern General Hospital as a captain in the Royal Army Medical Corps. He died in 1933.

Training in medical schools

By 1860, the old system of medical qualification by apprenticeship had largely been replaced by a more formal and consistent medical education made up of a defined syllabus, lectures and written examinations. In the first half of the nineteenth century, the vast majority of British doctors with a medical degree were educated in Scotland. This was because the ancient universities of Edinburgh, Glasgow, Aberdeen and St Andrews all had well-established medical schools, while the first of the new London medical schools did not open until 1821.

As demand increased, so did the number of medical schools in London. By 1841, St George's had 200 pupils, while St Bartholomew's Hospital had 300, with hundreds more students at the other London hospital schools. An added bonus was that London had a teaching university with two colleges, King's and University, which both had medical faculties. By 1858, twelve of London's hospitals had medical schools.

Medical students at the provincial hospital-based medical schools were entitled to take the examinations for the University of London, thereby qualifying for the university degrees of MB (Bachelor of Medicine), ChB (Bachelor of Surgery), CM (Master of Surgery) or MD (Doctor of Medicine).

From the 1840s, Oxford and Cambridge medical students went to London or elsewhere to undertake two or three years of clinical work because the larger cities had hospitals offering comprehensive clinical training. They then returned to their universities to be examined and qualify for the Cambridge or Oxford medical degrees. After the 1860s, medical students could study at other provincial centres such as Bristol and Manchester, as an alternative to Oxbridge and the Scottish cities.

By 1908, prospective medical students had to pass a preliminary examination and register with the General Medical Council before commencing study at university. They could be as young as 16. The minimum length of the course was five years, but it could stretch to six or seven if the various examinations were not passed first time.

In the same year, *Jack's Reference Book* by T C and E C Jack estimated the total cost of five years' medical training to be from about £600 to £1,000, the higher limit applying if the student qualified at one of the older universities. The cost of medical training could be reduced if the student lived at home or he was able to win a scholarship to one of the medical schools. Books and apparatus were estimated at between £40 and £50, and lodgings from £60 to £100 a year if the student could not live at home. Examination fees were extra.

THOMAS TURNER, SURGEON

The youngest child of a banker, Thomas Turner was born in Truro, Cornwall, in 1793. Having decided on a medical career, he was apprenticed to Nehemiah Duck, a surgeon at St Peter's Hospital in Bristol. In 1815, he became a student at Guy's and St Thomas's Hospital in London and was a pupil of the eminent surgeon, Sir Astley Cooper. The following year, he became a licentiate of the Society of Apothecaries and a member of the Royal College of Surgeons. Thomas completed his medical education in Paris, where he stayed until 1817.

Thomas Turner, FRCS, c.1870. (Author's collection)

On returning to England, he settled in Manchester, where his married sister lived. Thomas was appointed as surgeon to the Manchester Workhouse but had to resign the post in 1820 because of ill-health. He set up a private practice in Manchester and from 1822 became well-known as a lecturer on anatomy and physiology. According to his entry in the *Oxford Dictionary of National Biography* by Stella Butler, in 1824, Thomas 'transferred his lecture course to a house in Pine Street and set about organising a school of medicine where students could gain experience of dissection as well as attend a range of lecture courses.' The Pine Street School of Medicine became known as 'the first complete provincial school of medicine'. It became recognised by the Society of Apothecaries and the Royal College of Surgeons of Edinburgh, and later by the Royal College of Surgeons of England.

Plarr's Lives of the Fellows of the Royal College of Surgeons of England points out that Thomas Turner helped to 'break up the monopoly of medical education possessed by the London Schools at the beginning of the nineteenth century', showing that large provincial towns were 'capable of affording a first-rate medical education'.

Thomas was appointed surgeon to the Deaf and Dumb Institution in 1825, and five years later, he obtained the same post at the Manchester Royal Infirmary. Turner's Pine Street School merged with the medical school at Chatham Street in 1859, becoming the Royal School of Medicine. In 1872, it became the medical faculty of Owens College, Manchester.

Thomas Turner's entry in the *Medical Register* simply records his qualification as 'Fell R Coll Surg Eng 1843', proving that he was one of the first 600 elected fellows to the college. His earlier medical qualifications in 1816 are not mentioned, nor are they included in the *Medical Directory*. This is yet another example that highlights the importance of tracking down obituaries where possible to back up and supplement the information obtained from other sources. Thomas Turner died in 1873 at the age of 81.

Women doctors

Although women had been unqualified medical practitioners for centuries – for instance, as midwives, abortionists or herbalists – it was not until the nineteenth century that they started fighting for the right to be qualified doctors on the same footing as men. The battle was to be long and frustrating.

The first registered female doctor in Britain was Elizabeth Blackwell, who qualified in the USA in 1849. She was able to have her name included on the new *Medical Register* of 1859 because, at first, doctors with foreign degrees were allowed to register if they had been in practice in Britain before October 1858. Crucially, the sex of the doctor was not specified. In *The Excellent Doctor Blackwell*, Julia Boyd notes that Elizabeth's prior contact with the president of the General Medical Council was probably of paramount importance because her medical practice in Britain 'amounted to little more than a few consultations'.

This loophole was very quickly closed so that no other women could be admitted to the *Register* until 1865. The name which was added in that year was Elizabeth Garrett, the first woman to qualify as a doctor in Britain. She, too, had to exploit legal loopholes to make progress. Although she had applied to numerous teaching hospitals and universities, she was turned down by them all except for a short period in 1860–61 when she studied at the Middlesex Hospital in London.

After threat of legal action, the Society of Apothecaries ruled that if Elizabeth completed a period of study under private tuition from teachers at recognised medical schools and served an apprenticeship under a licensed apothecary, it could not refuse to let her take its examinations. Elizabeth duly became a licentiate of the Society of Apothecaries in 1865, and secured her place on the *Medical Register*. She quickly developed an extensive private practice, and in 1866 set up the St Mary's Dispensary for Women in Marylebone. By 1870, she had obtained a medical degree from the University of Paris, the first woman to do so.

The following year, Elizabeth set up the New Hospital for Women above the dispensary, which was to be staffed only by women. In 1874, she also helped to set up the London School of Medicine for Women. Unusually for the time, Elizabeth's marriage in 1871 to the wealthy ship-owner James Anderson and subsequent motherhood did not halt her career.

In 1868, the Society of Apothecaries ruled that it would only accept candidates for its examinations who were enrolled at recognised medical schools. This effectively closed the route through which Elizabeth Garrett had qualified, making it yet more difficult for other women to follow her example. The difficulties women faced appeared to be insurmountable: in addition to the general prejudice against women in the medical profession, there was a distinct absence of institutions offering a medical education to female students, and a lack of colleges or universities offering degrees to them.

While some British women had gone abroad to obtain medical degrees at the universities of Zurich and Berne, Sophia Jex-Blake campaigned for the same opportunities to be available in Britain. Sophia's approach was more public and aggressive, in sharp contrast to Blackwell and Garrett, who were both known for quiet tact and diplomacy.

In 1869, in response to her application to study there, Edinburgh University informed Sophia that it was not practical to hold separate classes for one woman (as she would not be allowed to join the men's classes). Sophia promptly found four other women, all wanting to study medicine, and they signed the matriculation roll on 2 November. They became the first female medical students to attend a British university. By the end of the first year, two more women had joined and they became known as the 'Edinburgh Seven'.

There was increasing opposition to the group, and in 1871 they were refused entry to the Edinburgh Royal Infirmary where the medical students obtained their clinical training. It was not until 1873 that the women received limited access to the wards.

Despite this, in 1872, the university court ruled that even if female students completed their medical training and passed all the examinations, it could not grant them degrees. Sophia Jex-Blake appealed to the Scottish Court of Session and the university's decision was overturned. Edinburgh University appealed to a higher court and eight months later, their original ruling was upheld. The women were effectively expelled from the university.

In response, Sophia founded the London School of Medicine for Women, which opened in October 1874 with fourteen students, including Sophia herself. A group of distinguished male medical practitioners agreed to give lectures, but the school was not recognised by any of the nineteen licensing bodies so its students could not be examined. It was also not affiliated with any hospital of 150 beds or more where the students could gain their clinical training.

Meanwhile, Elizabeth Blackwell started a lobby group to promote legislation to solve the problem of women qualifying in medicine. Her old friend Russell Gurney, MP, drafted a Private Member's Bill to deal with the issue. On 11 August 1876, the Russell Gurney Enabling Bill became law, which simply stated that all nineteen of the medical examining bodies could accept women as candidates, although they could not be compelled to do so.

This clarification of the law encouraged several of the licensing bodies to admit women, and the King's and Queen's College of Physicians in Dublin was the first to do so later that year. In addition, on 15 March 1877, the London Free Hospital became affiliated to the London School of Medicine for Women – for the first time, female medical students were entitled to both medical training and registration in Britain.

By 1891, there were 101 registered female doctors in Britain and this number rose to 477 twenty years later. Some women who had qualified as nurses before the end of the nineteenth century went on to qualify as doctors. Once qualified, many female doctors worked in local authority services or in women's or children's hospitals, which were, without doubt, areas of the profession in which there was less competition with men. Large numbers of women doctors, however, built up successful private practices.

By 1908, most British universities, except Oxford and Cambridge, allowed women to take their degrees. The London Society of Apothecaries and the Conjoint Board of the Royal College of Physicians and Surgeons admitted women to their examinations for diplomas, including surgery and dentistry.

There were women-only medical schools at the London (Royal Free Hospital) School of Medicine, the Medical College for Women at Edinburgh and the Queen Margaret College in Glasgow. Scholarships were available to women candidates at the London Royal Free Hospital, Owens College in Manchester and the Queen Margaret College in Glasgow.

ANN ELIZABETH CLARK, MD

Dr Ann Elizabeth Clark, c.1910.
(Courtesy of *The Friend*)

As the daughter of a Quaker (a religion committed to female education), it is perhaps not surprising that Ann Elizabeth Clark should have had a successful career. She was born in 1844, the fifth daughter of James Clark of Street, Somerset, who, with his brother, was a successful manufacturer of sheepskin rugs, boots and shoes. Ann was educated at a private school in Bath but did not start to study medicine until her late twenties. She joined Sophia Jex-Blake and a small group of other women students at Edinburgh, and when they were forced to leave, she enrolled with them at the newly opened London School of Medicine for Women in 1874.

Instead of waiting for the opportunity to take a medical qualification in Britain, Ann went to Switzerland to study at the German-speaking University of Berne. In 1877, she obtained the degree of MD, Berne. The following year, she became a licentiate of the College of Physicians, Ireland, which had opened its doors to women in 1876. She became a licentiate of King's and Queen's College of Physicians of Ireland in 1878 and was also awarded the LM (licentiate in midwifery) in the same year.

According to her obituary in *The Friend*, after qualifying, Ann 'spent some time in special medical work in Paris and Vienna, and in Boston, U.S.A.' Ann's medical training, in Britain and abroad, would have been expensive, but it is believed that after her father retired in the 1860s, she received regular funds from the Clarks' business.

On her return to Britain, Ann's first post was as resident medical officer to the Birmingham and Midland Hospital for Women, to which she was appointed in 1878; later, she fulfilled the same role at the Children's Hospital until around 1882. Ann then set up a successful private practice in Edgbaston, Birmingham.

She was appointed honorary physician to both the Women's and Children's Hospitals, and, according to the *British Medical Journal*, she made 'a specialty of the diseases of women and children; and was not only trusted, but beloved by all her patients'. She regularly worked with Lawson Tait as his anaesthetist at a time when he was undertaking his pioneering abdominal and gynaecological surgery.

Ann retired in 1913, moving back to her birthplace of Street, Somerset, to live with her sister. She was able to enjoy travel in her retirement, visiting Italy, Greece and Switzerland, but became increasingly infirm in her later years. Ann died in February 1924 at the age of 80.

Birmingham Children's Hospital. (Author's collection)

Chapter 3

PLACES OF WORK

Getting established

After completing his medical apprenticeship or university degree, the newly qualified surgeon, apothecary or physician began his struggle for recognition and financial success. There were several options open to him. He could become a salaried assistant to an established practitioner, set up his own practice or go into partnership with another. He could also apply for a position in one of the city or county hospitals, but competition for these posts was fierce.

The dispensary of the London Hospital. (*The Sphere*, 13 June 1903)

If he only wanted to practise as an apothecary and not as a surgeon-apothecary or general practitioner, he could set up his own shop or apply for a post as a salaried dispenser in a hospital, although these positions were rare and therefore highly sought after.

Private practice

It was not until the 1820s that the term 'general practitioner' (GP) came into use. Newly qualified medical men struggled financially at the beginning of their careers, and if they set up in practice by themselves, it could take a number of years before a practitioner was established and successful, if at all. The decision about where to set up in practice was usually a tactical one. Ambitious young practitioners might gravitate towards towns and cities with large hospitals – in the hope of future work there, either in a house position or as an honorary consultant later in their careers. Conversely, such men might compete for patients with the very hospitals they aspired to be associated with. Rural areas did not offer such lucrative practices, although practitioners sometimes returned to the area in which their family lived, to work in their local community.

A private practice was usually run from a doctor's own house unless he could afford separate consulting rooms, and in most towns there was a 'medical district' in which the most successful practitioners lived. Many of the properties in these districts, which were well-known as places where doctors practised, had valuable goodwill associated with them. Areas of longstanding medical practice are evident in the street names and buildings of such localities: Doctor's Hill, Doctor's Close or simply 'the doctor's house'.

Less successful members of the medical profession, or those just starting to establish themselves, would not have had eminent physicians or surgeons as their neighbours. No matter where a medical professional set up in private practice, he or she needed a library, transport and domestic servants, in addition to a consulting room.

Marrying the master's daughter was a common way to kick-start a medical career, with the newly qualified surgeon or surgeon-apothecary entering into partnership with his father-in-law. Equally, father-and-son partnerships were a valuable way to keep a hard-won professional reputation in the family. Physicians, however, always went into practice by themselves.

For private practice, most established practitioners employed one or two assistants who could be either resident or non-resident, and qualified or unqualified. This was especially the case if the practitioner had a surgery attached to his home. According to Charles Booth in *Life and Labour of the People in London*, resident indoor qualified assistants were paid between £60 and £100 a year, and between £30 and £60 a year if unqualified. Outdoor assistants usually had 'their rooms found for them by the principal, and earn £80 to £150 when qualified, and £50 to £80 if unqualified'.

Working as a salaried assistant in this way could be a useful stepping stone for the newly qualified medical practitioner. The experience he gained in the day-to-day running of a practice, including the business side of it, was invaluable when it came to setting up on his own.

With the introduction of the National Insurance Act of 1911, workers on low pay received free healthcare and the workload of GPs increased considerably. According to Geoffrey Rivett on his National Health Service History website (www.nhshistory.net), 1,000 insurance patients generated an income of around £400–£500 a year, supplemented by fee-paying non-insurance patients. By the 1920s, GPs were seriously overstretched, especially in inner city areas. In 1948, they became linchpins of the new National Health Service (NHS).

Hospitals

There was always stiff competition when a post as a medical officer in a well-regarded hospital became vacant. When such posts were advertised in the local and national press, and in medical journals such as the *Lancet* and the *British Medical Journal*, applications came from far and wide, since it was expected that moving to another part of the country was necessary to progress in a medical career.

The number and status of medical officers in a hospital depended on its size. As a bare minimum, each hospital had several honorary part-time consultants, employed on an unpaid basis, as well as a resident house surgeon who received a salary. In some larger hospitals such as the London, there was a house surgeon and a surgical registrar, while at other smaller institutions the role was combined.

Senior hospital consultants

As part of their duties, honorary consultants in teaching hospitals gave regular clinical lectures to the medical students who paid to attend them. The fees were shared by the consultants. They also 'walked the wards' with their medical students. Although they were unpaid, honorary consultants worked in hospitals for the prestige attached to such appointments, and the extra private practice which would come about as a result.

This part-time system of appointing honorary consultants continued well into the twentieth century. Afterwards, and especially in the years leading up to the founding of the NHS, consultants were paid generous honoraria.

Junior hospital posts

In 1860, there were approximately 15,000 registered medical practitioners. However, as Brian Abel-Smith points out in *The Hospitals 1800–1948: A Study in Social Administration in England and Wales*, fewer than 1,200 were working in 117 of the larger voluntary hospitals. The remainder worked as assistants and junior housemen, who chose the most interesting cases for their seniors from the out-patients department. Their daily duties included supervising their seniors' in-patients when they were not in the hospital, and they did the work previously carried out by apothecaries. The title of apothecary for the resident medical officer disappeared between the middle and third quarter of the nineteenth century.

According to W F Bynum in *Science and the Practice of Medicine in the Nineteenth Century*, resident medical officers had to do most of the teaching of medical students, who followed them on their rounds in the hospitals. In the early days, junior doctors were not paid; small annual salaries were introduced for resident medical officers, varying between £50 and £100 plus full board.

Resident staff had free board and lodging within the hospital, which usually included a separate sitting room and bedroom. All resident staff had to adhere to institutions' strict rules, or face censure or dismissal. These included not being absent without leave, and having to ask permission to be out of the hospital after a certain hour.

There were also a number of 'dressers' in every hospital, appointed by the surgical officers. Usually still students, these men paid for the privilege of working closely with eminent surgeons and had to attend daily when the surgeon visited the hospital. A major attraction of this 'apprenticeship' was that dressers could help in the operating theatre if required. They could perform minor operations in the presence of senior staff, but, despite their name, they were not allowed to put on or remove any dressings without supervision.

The armed services

Many newly qualified medical professionals chose to serve in the Royal Navy or British Army for a short period before settling down in private practice. For some, it became their lifelong career.

The British Army

Before 1858, a diploma from the Royal College of Surgeons or the equivalent from Edinburgh or Dublin was all that was needed for entry into the army medical service. Under the 1858 warrant reforms, new entrants were required to pass competitive examinations and have equal qualifications to that of a newly qualified civilian medical practitioner. This included a licence from the Royal College of Physicians plus the Royal College of Surgeons diploma, or equivalent. The 1867 warrant reinforced these entry requirements. After ten years of service, medical officers within the army could receive a gratuity or retire on half-pay.

During the Crimean War (1854–55), the army had to recruit large numbers of extra surgeons, often at short notice. Edward Wrench, who later became surgeon lieutenant colonel for the 2nd Volunteer Battalion of the Sherwood Foresters, recalled his experiences in the Crimea in an article in the *British Medical Journal* called 'The Lessons of the Crimean War'.

When Edward reached the Crimea, he was immediately given charge of between twenty and thirty patients, 'wounded from Inkermann, mixed with cases of cholera, dysentery and fever'. According to Edward, 'There were no nurses, no washing conveniences, either personal, or for clothing. Two old soldiers, called orderlies, did their ignorant best to attend to the wants of the patients, but were chiefly occupied in rude cooking and burying the dead.' Perhaps worst of all, there were very little medicines and even the base hospital at Balaclava had no opium, quinine or ammonia.

As part of their duties, assistant surgeons (never full surgeons) had to undertake regular trench duty, and during the winter one assistant surgeon accompanied each trench guard, who was relieved every twelve hours. After the winter, the trench guard and medical officers remained on duty twenty-fours a day, and with the increasing number of trenches, the number of assistant surgeons was increased correspondingly.

Edward Wrench recalled that until late in the siege, no shelter was provided for the surgeons and 'they had to brave the elements as well as the

shot and shell, and to attend the wounded in extraordinary circumstances ...'
He cited one example: 'On one occasion a shot killed two stretcher-bearers,
and took the leg off the patient while the surgeon was dressing him for a
previous wound.'

One young surgeon who experienced the horrors of the Crimean War first-
hand was Tertius Ball. He had qualified as a member of the Royal College of
Surgeons of England in 1850 and became a licentiate of the Society of
Apothecaries in 1852. His first appointment was as the assistant house
surgeon at Cardiff's Royal Infirmary. In their annual report for 1853/54, the
hospital governors recorded that they had granted 'leave to their late House
Surgeon, Mr Ball, to vacate his appointment at a short notice, in order to
enable him to accept medical service which had been offered him in the
Crimea'.

Tertius Ball appears to have found his niche in the army and continued
within the service after the war ended. The *Medical Register* records that he
received an MD degree from the University of St Andrews in 1862. At the
time, he was a staff assistant surgeon; five years later, he was promoted to
staff surgeon.

Hart's Army List of 1879 states that Tertius was now a surgeon major. He
had been appointed assistant surgeon on 3 November 1854 and surgeon on
8 June 1867. During this time, the *List* notes that he was working in Bengal.
Tertius was placed on half-pay on 12 March 1875, having served more than
twenty years in the army. This meant he had retired; on the 1881 census, he
was living in Tottenham with his wife Sophia, listed as a 'Retired Army
Surgeon'. He died the following year.

Horrendous conditions in the Crimean War and woefully inadequate
supplies and resources meant a drastic reorganisation of the army's medical
services was needed. In May 1854, the Hospital Conveyance Corps was
formed to carry the wounded on stretchers and drive wagons (in 1855, it was
renamed the Land Transport Corps). Before this, stretcher-bearing had been
carried out by pensioner volunteers.

In 1855, the Medical Staff Corps was founded by royal warrant specifically
for service in hospitals (replaced a year later by the Army Hospital Corps).
From 1857, being literate was a requirement for all members of the Army
Hospital Corps – an important point given the fact that they handled drugs
and needed to read instructions from medical staff.

Before 1873, surgeons joining the army were attached to individual
regiments, but after this date they became part of the medical staff of the

A Red Cross ambulance car with Royal Army Medical Corps soldiers. (The Sphere, 7 November 1914)

Army Medical Department. Surgeons were still not ranked as officers: technically, they had no power to command the orderlies of the Army Hospital Corps. Working for the army was seen very much as second best to posts in hospitals, or even general practice.

The Royal Army Medical Corps (RAMC)

The situation did not improve until the formation of the Royal Army Medical Corps (RAMC) in 1898. From this date, surgeons were given equal status and rank with other army officers, although their salaries remained lower.

By the 1890s, prospective army medical officers had to pass a highly competitive examination before undergoing a rigorous course of training and lectures at the Royal Victoria Hospital at Netley, 'with special applications to the exigencies of army life'.

The RAMC consisted of officers with permanent commissions, supplemented by others on temporary commissions. During the First and Second World Wars, civilian doctors were called up or volunteered to join the RAMC, holding temporary officer rank during the time they served in the army. They were not included in the *Army List*.

ALBERT MORRELL, RAMC

Private Albert Morrell, RAMC (right), outside the Embarkation Medical Stores, Suez, c.1943. (Courtesy of Paul Morrell)

In the First and Second World Wars, non-medically trained men could volunteer to join the Royal Army Medical Corps (RAMC) to work as nursing orderlies. Albert Morrell was one such Second World War recruit. Married with two children, he was a trolley-bus conductor from Derby. On 13 March 1941, he enlisted at No. 11 Depot and Training Establishment, RAMC, Beckett Park, Leeds and became 7395556 Private Albert Morrell, RAMC.

In each platoon at Beckett Park, there were thirty men housed in one block, where they also ate. Albert joined other recruits undertaking a special intensive course of training in technical subjects, which lasted for around six weeks. Subjects covered included: drill, dentistry, basic nursing training and even how to take casualties across water. Unlike other units, the RAMC course did not include battle training and only one route march of around twenty miles was required during the training.

After completing the course, each man had a few days' leave before being issued with his posting orders. Technically, they could be sent to any army unit, usually as a nursing orderly. While at the depot, Albert would have been kitted out with a uniform for overseas service, and received inoculations against tropical diseases.

Albert completed his training on 15 May 1941 and was posted to No. 1 Depot, RAMC, Boyce Barracks near Aldershot, which was the RAMC's base depot, on 8 August. There, he would have received further training in first aid, including bandaging and treating wounds, burns and snake bites, as well as the use of antiseptics, sterilising instruments for operating and the identification of certain gases.

On 27 October 1941, Albert left Aldershot bound for the troopship, the *Oronsay*, which was waiting in Greenock on the Clyde estuary. After travelling in the USS *West Point* convoy to Cape Town via Nova Scotia and Trinidad, Albert's long journey continued to India, where he was sent to the Deolali transit camp, 150 miles north of Bombay. New recruits to the RAMC depot that were sent overseas without being attached to a particular unit went to Deolali before being posted on to other units in India, the Middle East or South East Asia.

In early 1942, Albert was returned to Bombay and boarded the same transport ship he had disembarked from, the *West Point*, this time bound for Singapore. Luckily for him, the *West Point* was one of the transport ships that took civilian evacuees to Colombo before returning to Bombay – he was therefore not part of the force that landed in Singapore, which became involved in heavy fighting before being ordered to surrender as Japanese prisoners of war.

From Bombay, Albert was sent to Suez in Egypt where he was posted to HQ 80 Sub Area Suez. Like the other troops and service personnel in the Suez Canal area, Albert lived under canvas for much of the time.

Albert served on the staff of the embarkation medical officer (EMO), based at the Sub Depot Medical Stores, 13 British General Hospital (BGH) Suez. The EMO carried out medical examinations of troops in transit and dealt with any health problems found among them (including cases of infectious diseases). He also dispersed casualties on newly arrived ships and supervised the embarkation of casualties being evacuated to India or South Africa; replenishing the medical supplies of troopships and hospital ships calling at the port was another duty.

Albert's daily work involved driving casualties from place to place, and delivering medical supplies to the ships which needed them. His war was cut short on 5 April 1944 when he was involved in a serious road accident, in which he fractured his left femur and left radius. After spending thirty-three days at 13 BGH Suez, he was transferred to No. 2 Orthopaedic Centre, 63rd General Hospital Heliopolis in Cairo. He returned home on the hospital ship *Oranje* in August 1944.

In Britain, he was sent to four different hospitals and was finally discharged on 27 March 1945, but the long-lasting effects of his injuries meant that he could not return to work as a bus conductor. Instead, he worked as a semi-skilled light labourer, although in August 1945 he fractured his left leg again. In 1948, Albert successfully appealed for a war pension under the Pensions Appeal Tribunals Act of 1943, arguing that if he had been fit and well on leaving the army, he could have expected to be promoted to be a bus driver at 100s. whereas the wage rate as a labourer was 91s. 6d.

(With grateful thanks to Paul Morrell for the above information about his grandfather, taken from his unpublished work 'Albert's War'.)

The Royal Navy

At first, the medical care offered to sick and injured sailors was minimal, both at sea and ashore. Barber-surgeons worked on board Tudor warships, but it is not known when this became standard practice. Sailors needing medical attention were often billeted in inns and taverns at the next port of call, to be tended by the local surgeon. It became clear that naval hospitals were required in Britain to provide a higher standard of care.

The first hospital exclusively for naval patients was requisitioned at Plymouth in 1689, followed by further ones in other ports. Finally, in 1753, the first purpose-built naval hospital was opened at Haslar near Gosport. From the seventeenth century onwards, there were therefore two areas of work open to surgeons in the Royal Navy: serving on a ship and working in a navy hospital ashore.

As the eighteenth century was one of almost continuous warfare, surgeons were in great demand. By then, every candidate wishing to be appointed as a surgeon or surgeon's mate (later termed 'assistant surgeon') had to pass a qualifying examination at Surgeons' Hall in London, administered by the Company of Surgeons, and later the Royal College of Surgeons.

There was one surgeon and one surgeon's mate per ship. These medical officers had to deal with injuries caused by war, as well as the extremely prevalent tropical diseases that regularly beset the sailors, including yellow fever, dysentery and malaria. They were assisted by 'loblolly boys' – fellow seamen and marines, who either volunteered or were detailed to do the work – named after the porridge they fed to the invalids.

After the peace in 1783, the number of naval surgeons, which had doubled during the war, was drastically reduced, with large numbers leaving the service. From 1805, every new ship had a 'sick berth' compartment, thereby improving conditions on board for those needing medical treatment. In 1827, another naval hospital, the Melville at Chatham, opened to cope with increased demand.

The expansion of overseas trade meant that the Royal Navy needed 'hospital' stations abroad, and these were established in 1833 in Malta, Jamaica, Bermuda and Simonstown. At the same time, around forty 'sick

---

ARCHIBALD LESLIE ARCHER, MD

As he was born in Devonport, perhaps it is not surprising that Archibald Leslie Archer should have made his career from the sea. He qualified in 1849 and joined the Royal Navy on 28 February 1860.

The *Navy List* records that Archibald served on the sloop *416 Rinaldo S.* in 1864, which sailed to North America and the West Indies. In 1865 and 1866, he was serving as an additional surgeon on *262 Indus*, a guard ship of the Reserve (2,098 tons), flag ship of the Admiral Superintendent, Devonport. By 1869, he was on board the *113 Clio* which went to the Pacific, but was subsequently ordered home.

Archibald Archer appears on the 'Surgeons Retired' list by 1870. The censuses for 1871, 1881, 1891 and 1901 bear this out. Archibald was living in Stoke Damerel, Devonport, listed as a 'Doctor of Medicine Retired Staff Surgeon RN'.

quarters' were set up in Britain. A 'sick berth attendant' category of naval rating was set up, with different rates of pay for assistant sick berth attendants, sick berth attendants and sick berth stewards.

Within the Royal Navy, there was a defined career structure, starting with surgeons, staff surgeons and fleet surgeons. One of the attractions of serving as a naval medical officer was that it was possible to progress through the ranks, with an increase in salary accompanying each promotion; another was the pension or gratuity on retirement. By 1908, the Royal Navy paid their surgeons between £255 and £310 per annum, staff surgeons from £365 to £438 and fleet surgeons from £493 to £657.

The Honourable East India Company and the Indian Army

From the beginning of the seventeenth century until the Indian Mutiny (1857–59), doctors were in demand to work for the Honourable East India Company. Granted a charter in 1600, the company held a monopoly on all English trade east of the Cape of Good Hope. Surgeons could serve on board the company's ships, known as 'East Indiamen', or ashore at one of the trading posts in India. The company's main role from 1833 was as the British government's imperial agent in India.

Employees of the company were able to take advantage of lucrative trading opportunities and amass vast fortunes. Elgin-born Alexander Gray was a surgeon for the East India Company in Bengal for more than twenty years. When he died in India in 1807, he left most of his wealth to his home town, including £20,000 to build a hospital, which became known as Dr Gray's Hospital.

The Indian Army was another overseas branch which needed doctors, starting in 1861 and going through to partition in 1947. The Indian Medical Service was the collective name given to the top ranks of the East India Company/Indian Army's medical service. Until 1896, it was divided into three administrative divisions: Bengal, Bombay and Madras; from 1897, these divisions were combined into one general service.

The Poor Law service

If a qualified doctor had been unable to secure a position in a hospital, he could apply for a post within the Poor Law service as a resident workhouse medical officer. He could also be appointed as a district Poor Law medical officer, and he would have to carry out the associated duties for this in addition to his general practice. In 1844, one in six doctors held posts in the Poor Law service.

At first, the guardians of the Poor Law unions, who ran the workhouses, treated the medical officers like tradesmen who supplied goods for the institutions, inviting bids for the lowest contract. It was not until 1842 that the Poor Law Board ruled that medical officers in England and Wales should receive a salary.

In any case, high standards were insisted upon. Applicants for the post of both workhouse medical officer and district medical officer needed a diploma or degree as a surgeon from a royal college or university in England, Scotland or Ireland. In addition, they needed a degree in medicine *or* a diploma or licence from the Royal Physicians of London *or* a certificate to practise as an apothecary from the Society of Apothecaries of London. They could also apply if they had been in practice as an apothecary on 1 August 1815, or if they had a warrant or commission as surgeon or assistant surgeon in the Royal Navy, the British Army or the Honourable East India Company prior to 1 August 1826.

In Scotland, legislation in 1845 had decreed that doctors should be on the staff of the poorhouses. However, according to Steven Cherry in *Medical Services and the Hospitals in Britain 1860–1939*, as late as the 1890s, almost 10 per cent of parishes still paid general practitioners for individual visits and services for the poor.

The main duty of the resident workhouse medical officer was to examine the paupers as they were admitted to the receiving ward. If any paupers were found to be ill, the medical officer had to direct the master to put them in the sick ward. He also had to decide if paupers of unsound mind were fit to stay in the workhouse, or whether they were too dangerous to themselves and others, and therefore should be sent to a lunatic asylum.

Throughout the nineteenth century and into the twentieth, the guardians of Poor Law unions relied on the workhouse medical officers to supply drugs for the inmates from their own salaries, which was an extremely contentious issue. Medical officers often recommended extras like food and beer to provide nourishment for the sick paupers under their care. As these extras were part of the workhouse diet, they did not have to be funded from the medical officers' own pockets.

In London by 1888, workhouse infirmaries were run by superintendents who had often previously been resident housemen in voluntary hospitals.

Each superintendent had on his staff a full-time assistant medical officer. According to Brian Abel-Smith, by 1905 the annual salaries of these London Poor Law union superintendents were between £350 and £500, with accommodation, coal, gas and laundry thrown in as extra benefits. Extra fees were available for certifying lunatics and for vaccinations.

There was little incentive to stay within the Poor Law medical service as working conditions and pay were not comparable with those of the voluntary hospitals.

Junior medical assistants were paid £100 per annum while the starting annual salary of senior assistants was £120, which could rise to a maximum of £160. Staff turnover was therefore high and assistant medical officers rarely stayed for longer than a few years.

Lunatic asylums

Working as a medical officer or asylum superintendent at a lunatic asylum was another option open to qualified medical professionals. Aside from the usual medical diplomas, there were no special qualifications required. Usually, applicants had developed an interest in the treatment of the insane while training or in their first hospital post. In 1886, the Medico-Psychological Association introduced the Certificate in Psychological Medicine, which was the first specific post-graduate qualification for psychiatry.

While being in charge of the medical care for a large institution like an asylum offered an attractive salary, there was one problem: by their very nature, the posts were residential and accommodation was often within the asylum building itself.

When Robert Jamieson, consulting physician to the Royal Lunatic Asylum in Aberdeen died in 1895, the *Lancet* described him as Scotland's 'oldest asylum superintendent'. Born in the city in 1818, Robert studied medicine in Edinburgh, and the *Medical Register* records that he gained his MD degree in 1839 and became a licentiate of the Royal College of Surgeons of Edinburgh in the same year.

Robert was appointed as medical superintendent to Aberdeen's Royal Lunatic Asylum in 1840. His obituary notes that when he got married in 1846, he resigned from his post and moved into private practice. However, seven years later, he was unanimously re-elected, 'with accommodation according to his requirements'. The standard accommodation was obviously unsuitable for a married couple, perhaps being within the asylum itself. It is likely that the new accommodation was separate from the asylum, but within the grounds.

The *Lancet* mentions that Robert Jamieson, along with Dr Hutchings of Glasgow, was credited with introducing the non-restraint system in Scotland. This was put into action at Aberdeen and in his first medical report, which appears in the asylum's annual report of 1840, Robert explained his methods: '... we act on the principle of non-restraint as far as the construction and economy of the establishment will allow; ... threatening and abusive language and harsh measures of every description are not only found to be unnecessary but are strictly prohibited among the attendants and made the occasion of reprimand or dismissal when discovered.'

While in private practice, Robert Jamieson was lecturer on the practice of medicine and medical jurisprudence, and medical examiner for degrees at King's College, Aberdeen. This is mentioned in his entry in the *Medical Directory*, as is the publication of his work 'Lectures on the Medical Jurisprudence of Insanity', which, according to the *Lancet*, was held in high regard.

Robert Jamieson held his post at Aberdeen Asylum until 1881, when Dr William Reid was appointed to assist him. The *Lancet* notes that he retired from active responsibility in 1884, but remained as consulting physician. He died in 1895 at the age of 77.

Prisons

Newly qualified doctors could also apply for a post as medical officer in a prison. Such posts carried a huge volume of work, both medical and clerical, so it was not for the faint-hearted. The duties included examining new arrivals, those in punishment cells and those undertaking hard labour, as well as inspecting all the prisoners weekly.

On top of his medical duties, the prison medical officer had to write weekly reports for the governor and keep a journal of all his observations, including an inspection of the prison itself every three months. In addition, he had to provide medical treatment for the officers and prison employees, as well as their families, and examine all candidates for employment at the prison. One attraction of working in the prison service was that under the 1865 Prison Act superannuation allowances were provided on retirement.

Medical officers of health (MOHs)

Although the Public Health Act had been passed in 1848, it was not until 1872 that it was made compulsory for local authorities to appoint a medical officer of health (MOH). Some enlightened councils had done so years earlier, such as Liverpool in 1847, but most waited until they were compelled by law. At first, the medical officers were under-valued and poorly paid, and until 1875 it was not even necessary to be medically qualified to be an MOH. According to Stephen Halliday in *The Great Filth*, in that year the medical officers of Lincoln and Hampstead received annual salaries of £15 and £50 respectively, at a time when 'a town clerk could expect to be paid £2,000.'

In addition to the usual medical qualifications, it became standard practice for medical professionals who were applying for a post as a medical officer of health to have passed the Diploma in Public Health (DPH) as a post-graduate qualification. By 1908, according to *Jack's Reference Book*, medical officers in large districts were well paid, with salaries ranging from £350 to over £1,000. Those in smaller districts combined private practice with their public-health work in order to augment their smaller salaries.

Supplementary work for those in general practice

Unless doctors had an extremely successful private practice in a lucrative area, they had to supplement their income by doing other medical work. As the nineteenth century progressed, there were increasing opportunities to do so. Two of these have already been mentioned: working as an MOH and as a Poor Law medical officer. However, there were a myriad of other ways to generate extra income too.

The growing number of sick clubs and friendly societies in Victorian Britain were a form of insurance for members of the working classes who were in steady employment. Each club/society needed a qualified doctor to provide medical services when called for. Collieries, mills and factories often employed surgeons to deal with sickness or accidents amongst their workforces, and/or to examine the medical fitness of apprentices. Police surgeons were required to medically examine police staff and prisoners, and to carry out post-mortems on victims of murder, unexplained deaths, etc., and to present their findings at coroners' inquests or criminal trials.

JOHN MCNAB BALLENDEN

DEATH OF DR. BALLENDEN, OF
SEDGLEY.
We regret to record the death of Dr. John MacNab
Ballenden, of Bleak House, Sedgley, which occurred on
Thursday afternoon, at the ripe old age of 85 or 86
years. The deceased gentleman has resided in Sedgley,
and has had an extensive practice in the district for
over half a century. Some years ago he was medical
officer of health to Sedgley Local Board, and when he
resigned the office he was succeeded by Dr. Walker,
whose office was subsequently bestowed upon Dr.
Biggam. Until about six or seven months ago the late
doctor was medical officer and vaccination officer to
the Dudley Board of Guardians for Sedgley (No.
1.) district, but he retired on account of ill-
health and infirmity, and Dr. Powell received the
appointments. Within a comparatively short period we
believe Dr. Ballenden was certifying surgeon under the
Factory Acts for the district of Sedgley, the office now
being filled by Dr. Johnson, of Woodsetton. The
deceased gentleman was a familiar figure in the neighbourhood, and he will be greatly missed. At the weekly
meeting of the Board of Guardians yesterday, the chair-
man (Mr. J. Hughes) referred to the death of Dr.
Ballenden, who he said was the oldest officer of the
union, and who discharged his duties very satisfactorily.
He moved that a letter of condolence be forwarded to
his widow and family.—Mr. J. Law seconded, and the
motion was carried.

Obituary for John McNab Ballenden in the Dudley Herald, 1894. (Courtesy of Dudley Archives and Local History Service)

John McNab Ballenden was a doctor in general practice who undertook a number of other medical roles. He was born in Stromness, Orkney, in 1813. The *Medical Register* records that he became a licentiate of the Faculty of Physicians and Surgeons of Glasgow in 1847. He obtained his MD from the University of St Andrews in 1850 and became a licentiate of the Society of Apothecaries in London in the same year.

It is not known why John chose to settle in Staffordshire but he commenced general practice in Sedgley. The *Medical Directory* states that he had a number of additional appointments. He was a member of the Hunterian Society, a Poor Law medical officer, a police surgeon, a certifying factory surgeon and a medical referee for the London & Liverpool Assurance Society.

John's long association with the Dudley Poor Law union began in November 1859 when he was appointed medical officer for the Upper Sedgley District (also known as No. 1 District). He had the difficult task of visiting paupers in their homes, to administer medical relief, across a wide, geographical area, at the same time as attending to patients from his own practice. It was often hard for district medical officers to meet such demand and, as a result, there were frequent complaints about non-attendance or neglect.

In April 1877, it was alleged that John McNab Ballenden had neglected his duties by 'not having given proper Medical Attention to … Mary Edwards during her confinement' and that she died as a result. The guardians suspended him while investigations were carried out. An inquest into Mary Edwards's death confirmed that she 'died from exhaustion, consequent upon the weak state of the Heart, the laceration of the peritoneum and Vagina consequent on the cross-birth and protracted Labour.'

John McNab Ballenden wrote to the guardians explaining his actions:

> I prescribed some opium Pills, and gave a Saline mixture with Tartrate of Antimony, and left the case in charge of a midwife, to whom I gave the necessary directions, and told her if any alteration took place, to send for me again. Having had a very extensive midwifery practice extending over many years and amounting to about 9000 Patients, the case presented no difficulty to me, it was one requiring time, and medicine to allay irritation and help natural relaxation ... During my evening Surgery hours I had been told that another Doctor was attending Mrs Edwards ...

If he had returned to attend to Mary Edwards, John Ballenden had intended to carry out a craniotomy procedure, something he termed 'breaking up the child'. He explained: 'I would not when it is necessary hesitate to sacrifice the child to save the Mother ... Any man of experience with common sense would say in such a case, use every means to increase the natural dilation and diminish the bulk of the object to be passed through.'

The guardians were satisfied with his explanation for not attending Mary Edwards a second time and his suspension was removed. He continued as the district medical officer for the First Sedgley District until 1894, when he resigned due to ill-health and infirmity, dying the following year.

Chapter 4

DEVELOPMENT OF THE MEDICAL PROFESSION

Anaesthetists

Until the introduction of anaesthetics in the 1840s, basic surgical work included drawing teeth, lancing boils, dressing wounds, treating syphilitic chancres and sores, and trussing up ruptures. Long or complicated internal operations on conscious patients were simply not possible, given the risk of death from shock.

Nitrous oxide was first prepared by Joseph Priestley in 1772 and its potential for use in surgery was recognised by Humphry Davy in 1800. He discovered that if a combination of nitrous oxide and ether was inhaled, the patient became light-headed and had a feeling of hilarity and euphoria, hence the term 'laughing gas'.

Ether was also being highlighted as an effective anaesthetic and it was used for the very first time by William E Clarke in New York in January 1842: he extracted a tooth while his patient was unconscious under ether. Four years later, a public operation took place on a patient anaesthetised with ether at Massachusetts General Hospital on 16 October. This was followed on 21 December by a similar public operation at University College Hospital in London that was performed by Robert Liston. He amputated a diseased thigh while his patient was unconscious under ether and called the anaesthetic method a 'Yankee dodge'.

A liquid called chloroform became a popular anaesthetic because it was more potent than ether, so that patients became unconscious more quickly. It was also non-explosive, unlike ether. On 19 January 1847, James Young Simpson of Edinburgh used chloroform for the first time as pain relief for a patient in labour. Six years later, Queen Victoria publicly endorsed chloroform when she made use of it during the birth of Prince Leopold. It was administered to her by John Snow, the first specialist anaesthetist.

Chloroform was not without its drawbacks. It was easy to give an overdose and there were known cases of death from liver failure as a result of its use. In *Anaesthesia and the Practice of Medicine: Historical Perspectives*, Keith Sykes

An anaesthetic (ether) being administered through a Clover inhaler, c.1880. (Courtesy of Dr Ian Paterson, Department of Anaesthesia, Northern General Hospital, Sheffield)

and John Bunker point out that 'in England the popularity of chloroform declined after the 1870s because of the high mortality rate', but it continued to be used in Scotland until the beginning of the twentieth century.

Until the Second World War, patients were usually anaesthetised with nitrous oxide, chloroform or ether. Some specialist anaesthetists used inhalers to control the concentration of vapour, but this was rare. The usual practice was to place a gauze-covered mask over the mouth and nose of the patient, and to drop the vapour onto it. The effect was not immediate and several assistants were always on hand to hold patients down while they progressed through the delirium stage before reaching surgical anaesthesia.

At first, the work of anaesthetists was not considered to be highly skilled and anaesthetics were administered by medical students, junior doctors or general practitioner anaesthetists. The latter worked in voluntary hospitals on an honorary basis for no salary. It was hoped that the prestige of their hospital appointments would lead to more work for their private practice.

When paying patients had operations in voluntary hospitals, the anaesthetist was entitled to a proportion of the surgeon's fee, but this could be as little as 5 per cent.

In fact, a specialist knowledge of heart and lung function was required in order to administer anaesthetics safely. The Association of Anaesthetists of Great Britain and Ireland was founded in 1932 by Doctor Henry W Featherstone, partly to raise standards and to increase the status of the profession. It also aimed to promote the development of anaesthesia, and to represent the interests of anaesthetists.

The association was heavily involved in the introduction of the Diploma in Anaesthesia (DA) in 1935, and in helping to train specialist anaesthetists for the armed forces during the Second World War. Its professional journal, *Anaesthesia*, was first published in 1946.

In 1947, the association instigated the founding of the Faculty of Anaesthetists of the Royal College of Surgeons in England (which became the independent Royal College of Anaesthetists in 1992). Before the advent of the National Health Service in 1948, the association was closely involved in negotiations at an early stage, and this meant that anaesthetists achieved a status equal to other hospital consultants in the NHS.

FRANCIS FISHER WADDY, ANAESTHETIST

Born in 1903, Francis (Frank) Fisher Waddy was the son of a Methodist minister. The *Medical Register* states that he qualified in 1927, having gained an MB and ChB from the University of Manchester. However, the *Medical Directory* tells us more about his career. His first hospital appointment was as house surgeon to the Royal Infirmary in Manchester, but he moved to Northampton in

Dr F F Waddy, consultant anaesthetist at Northampton General Hospital, 1974.
(Courtesy of *Northampton Chronicle & Echo*)

1929, where he set up in general practice. The *Medical Directory* also reveals that he was a fellow of the Royal Society of Medicine and a founder member of the anaesthesia section of the society.

In June 1929, Francis was appointed honorary anaesthetist to the Northampton General Hospital, under the proviso that he should not engage in any work other than his own speciality. As an honorary appointment, the post carried no salary so he had to rely on his private practice for an income. At this time, anaesthetists were entitled to a proportion of the surgeon's fee but payments were very small.

By January 1930, Francis had administered nitrous oxide and air analgesia for midwifery cases at the hospital for the first time. This became a welcome supplement to his income from ordinary surgical and dental work. Private patients who wished to have their babies delivered in hospital and asked for this treatment were admitted by the surgeon and turned over to Francis, on the understanding that if the delivery was abnormal, the surgeon would be called in and would charge his customary fee. With normal deliveries, Francis could keep the fee for himself.

The complex issue of fees arose again in the late 1930s, when the local authorities agreed to pay for operations on schoolchildren for the removal of adenoids and tonsils, and for midwifery cases at the nearby maternity home. The fees were paid to the hospital, which were then paid to the surgeon, after which the anaesthetist was meant to be paid. According to Francis Waddy's own book, *A History of Northampton General Hospital 1743 to 1948*, 'the payments were in fact so small and there was so much difficulty in sorting out for which cases the honorary anaesthetist had been called in that in the end the anaesthetist told both the ear, nose and throat surgeon and the gynaecological surgeon not to bother about them.'

During the Second World War, Francis's wife, Ethel Hunter Waddy, who was also a general practitioner, supported him in the department in the role of honorary clinical assistant. In 1948, Francis was awarded the FFARCS (Fellowship of the Faculty of Anaesthetists of the Royal College of Surgeons). He became a consultant anaesthetist at Northampton when the NHS was founded in the same year.

Francis retired in 1968 and was designated emeritus consultant anaesthetist. In 1974, the aforementioned *History of Northampton General Hospital* was published. Francis Fisher Waddy died in 1991.

(With thanks to Richard and David Waddy).

Dentists

Before the organisation of the dental profession in Britain, there were a large number of occupations offering the extraction of teeth as part of their work. These included barbers, blacksmiths, 'toothdrawers', itinerants and other quacks. At this stage, extracting bad teeth was the full extent of dental surgery.

In the seventeenth century, 'operators for the teeth' started to offer false teeth as well as extractions – a service which was clearly aimed at the rich. These dentures were made from walrus, elephant or hippopotamus ivory. From around 1750, operators for the teeth were describing themselves as 'dentists', advertising a more comprehensive range of services. They included the treatment of gum diseases, scaling, fillings, dentures, tooth whitening and transplants. The poor could not afford such sophisticated treatment and continued simply to have their teeth extracted by travelling toothdrawers and other quacks.

Birmingham's Dental School at Newhall Street, 1900. (Courtesy of the School of Dentistry, Birmingham)

Most of these 'dentists' had no medical training and learnt their skills during an apprenticeship. The dental profession sought to raise its status, organise itself and provide quality dental training. This was first provided in London, where the Dental Hospital of London was opened in 1858, followed by the National Dental Hospital a year later.

The Licence in Dental Surgery (LDS) was established by the Royal College of Surgeons of England in 1860. Dental schools and hospitals, such as the London School of Dental Surgery and Metropolitan School of Dental Science, were set up to provide training courses leading up to the LDS. Candidates had to be at least 21 years of age with four years' experience of dentistry, which could include the required three years' training in dental mechanics.

The first LDS courses were two years long, covering a wide range of surgical, dental and medical subjects, including anatomy, physiology, surgery, medicine, chemistry and metallurgy. As part of the training, students had to carry out two years of clinical work in the various departments of a dental hospital. After 1877, a practical element was introduced to the examination; before that, there was none. By 1879, the Royal College of Surgeons of Edinburgh, Glasgow and Ireland were awarding the LDS. From 1899, dental histology was added to the curriculum, and students had to pass a preliminary exam in chemistry. Birmingham University awarded the first Bachelor of Dental Surgery degree (BDS) in 1906.

One of the problems with the LDS was that it was not compulsory to have it to practise legally as a dentist. In the 1870s, leading dentists campaigned rigorously for legislation that would regulate the dental profession. The result was the 1878 Dentists Act, which set up a Register of Dentists and required those registered to have attained the LDS.

Like the 1858 Medical Act before it, the Dentists Act did not outlaw unregistered people from practising. However, unless they were registered, they could not call themselves a 'dentist' or 'dental practitioner' or charge for 'the performance of any dental operation or for any dental attendance or advice'. Surgeons, pharmacists and other medical professionals who were already carrying out dental work could, however, apply to join the Register of Dentists. Two years later, the British Dental Association was established.

At first, the passing of the 1878 Dentists Act barred women from the register, since they were refused entry to the dental schools and therefore could not qualify. Lilian Murray was the first woman in the UK to qualify as a dentist in 1895, having studied in Edinburgh, where women were admitted. English dental schools did not admit women to LDS courses for another twenty years.

Women who were already practising as dentists did the same as countless other practitioners who had not joined the register: they continued to practise but did not use the term 'dentist' or 'dental practitioner'. Unregistered dentists still outnumbered qualified ones at the end of the nineteenth century and into the twentieth.

Finally, in 1921, the Dentists Act decreed that entry to the dental profession was by qualifying examination only. This put the dentists on a similar footing to physicians, surgeons and apothecaries. Even so, medical professionals such as pharmacists could continue to offer dental services if they were considered competent to do so.

Unlike most other medical practitioners, dentists were inextricably linked with trade and business through their willingness to advertise their services. Newly qualified dental surgeons could set up in private practice and/or be involved with one of the new specialist dental hospitals.

With the rising status of the dental profession came increased responsibility for educating people about dental hygiene and disease prevention. In 1896, the School Dentists Society was set up with the aim of encouraging teachers to include the brushing of teeth in the daily school routine, producing wallcharts as teaching resources.

Although free and low-cost dental treatment was available at voluntary hospitals, and approved societies paid for such treatment for insured workers from 1911, it was not until the advent of the NHS that free dental services were available to all. A school dental service was introduced as well as priority treatment for expectant and nursing mothers, and young children. Demand for NHS dental treatment was so high that in the first nine months 33 million artificial teeth were produced. The cost was prohibitive so charges for dentures had to be introduced from 1951.

Gynaecologists

It was in the 1840s when gynaecology started to emerge as a precise science, and medical practitioners started to specialise in 'women's diseases'. Specialist women's hospitals started to appear in London and quickly spread to the provinces. By 1871, there were twelve such institutions, including the Hospital for Diseases of Women in Newcastle upon Tyne (1865), the Jessop Hospital for Women in Sheffield (1864) and the Birmingham and Midland Hospital for Women (1871). From the 1870s, voluntary general hospitals started to set up their own gynaecological wards and departments.

CHARLES HENRY FELIX ROUTH, GYNAECOLOGIST

Dr Charles Henry Felix Routh, gynaecologist, c.1900. (Author's collection)

Described in his obituary in the *British Medical Journal* as a 'veteran physician', Charles Henry Felix Routh was born in 1822 in Malta, where his father was commissary general. The *Provincial Medical Journal* notes that he started his education in Canada and came to England when he was 15. Being an accomplished Latin and Greek scholar, Charles originally entered University College, London, as an arts student, but transferred to the medical faculty in 1840.

It was at University College that he first developed an interest in obstetrics and gynaecology, and became Dr Murphy's first obstetric physician's assistant. The *Medical Register* records that he became a member of the Royal College of Surgeons of England in 1843, gained his MB degree in London in 1845 and became a member of the Royal College of Physicians of London in 1859.

Both the *Provincial Medical Journal* and the *British Medical Journal* contradict this by noting that he took the MB in 1844, followed by an MD in 1845. After qualifying, he travelled to Paris, Prague and Vienna, where he met Professor Sammelweiss, who was using aseptic techniques in midwifery in the lying-in hospitals where mortality rates were very high. This was a novel concept at the time, but Charles Routh was convinced of its value, and presented a paper before the Royal Medical and Chirurgical Society in 1848 about the causes of endemic puerperal fever in Vienna.

According to the *British Medical Journal*, Charles Routh had been in private practice for a few years before deciding to specialise in gynaecology. He was elected assistant physician at the Samaritan Free

Hospital in 1855 and was one of the founders of the Obstetrical Society of London in 1858, which was later merged into the British Gynaecological Society.

Charles Routh was a prolific writer and his entries in the *Medical Directory* record numerous published works, mainly on obstetrics and gynaecology. First published in 1860, his work *Infant Feeding and its Influence, or the Causes and Prevention of Infant Mortality* 'ran through three editions, and was also issued in the United States and translated into foreign languages.' He died in 1909 at the age of 87.

The kinds of disorders treated included ovarian and mammary tumours, menstrual problems and pelvic pain. Although the first ovariotomies took place in the 1850s, it was not until the late 1860s and early 1870s that they became accepted as a standard surgical procedure.

The Royal College of Obstetricians and Gynaecologists was not founded until 1929, so before this time there were no additional qualifications required to practise gynaecological skills, other than the usual medical qualifications – especially surgery. Practitioners usually developed an interest in the subject during training and decided to specialise.

Opticians

The first formal mention of opticians in Britain came in 1629 when the Company of Spectacle Makers of London was incorporated. The company sought to control those working as spectacle makers in the capital, in order to maintain high standards of quality. By the late eighteenth century, its influence was on the wane, and by the late Victorian period it had minimal control of the profession.

London's opticians, who produced high-quality spectacles, developed a reputation for precision, and were highly regarded in Europe. However, the medical profession had a general contempt for spectacles and despised their use up until the end of the nineteenth century. There was, though, a gradual introduction of systematic eye-testing at specialist hospitals such as Moorfields.

In the nineteenth century, opticians combined the selling of spectacles with the sale of scientific instruments such as telescopes and opera glasses. Some opticians were also involved in the jewellery, watch-making and photography trades.

Along with other emerging medical professions, opticians acutely felt the need to differentiate themselves from the hawkers and pedlars who had flooded the market with cheap spectacles. The profession's first journal, the *Optician*, appeared in 1891; four years later, the British Optical Association (BOA) was founded.

To raise standards, new members, from 1 June 1896, were required to pass an examination. Three different grades were available: 'optic' was the most basic (BOA), followed by 'dioptric' (DBOA), then 'ophthalmometric' (OBOA). Opticians could also be fellows of the BOA. From 1897, opticians could apply for diplomas from the Worshipful Company of Spectacle Makers.

The founders of the British Optical Association were clearly astute. As Margaret Mitchell points out in *The History of the British Optical Association 1895–1978*, 'it is truly remarkable that at a time when the optician was no more than an insignificant tradesman, a band of men could be so far-sighted as to see exactly what was required to transform a motley collection of shopkeepers into a professional body with all the appropriate ideals and characteristics.'

During the First World War, the BOA was involved in setting up the Army Spectacle Depot, which supplied more than one million pairs of spectacles and almost two million goggles, as well as artificial eyes for soldiers who had lost their sight in combat.

With the advent of the new National Insurance Acts, an additional-benefits scheme through approved societies offered dental and optical appliances to insured members. Qualified opticians were to be used.

As the standard of examinations was rising every year, the BOA introduced a preliminary exam in 1925 to ensure that the basic education of candidates was sufficient before working towards the other exams. New exams were introduced for dispensing opticians (1929), orthoptics (1939) and the fitting of contact lenses (1947). From the 1920s onwards, there was an increase in the number of provincial centres offering training for the exams.

From 1935, the diplomas of the National Association of Opticians, the Scottish Association of Opticians, and the then Institute of Chemist Opticians were recognised equally with those of the British Optical Association and the Worshipful Company of Spectacle Makers.

Despite these efforts to raise educational standards and increase the profession's status, there was still no register of opticians in Britain, and it remained legal for anyone to call themselves an optician.

There was continued opposition from the medical profession about the question of registration for opticians – as a result, the Opticians Act was not passed until 1958. The Act made it illegal for unqualified practitioners to carry out sight tests or dispense optical appliances, and also officially recognised the ability of opticians to use drugs, practise orthoptics, and prescribe and fit contact lenses.

Pharmacists, chemists and druggists

Pharmacists, who were usually known as chemists and druggists in the eighteenth and nineteenth centuries, dispensed drugs and medicines to the public from their shops. They were a separate group from apothecaries, who also dispensed medicines, but increasingly gave medical treatment as well. The eighteenth-century chemists' or druggists' shop-windows were adorned with delftware jars in blue and white, though by the nineteenth century, amber, green and blue bottles had taken their place. Larger, higher-class shops often had their own well-equipped laboratories. Smaller premises would usually have a back room for preparing and making up medicines.

By and large, the role of chemists and druggists included dispensing to patients of physicians, making up preparations from their own recipe books, selling a growing range of proprietary medicines, and selling or refilling family medicine chests, advising on dosage at the same time. They often had several diverse sidelines in the fields of chemistry, food and health: for instance, cupping (a form of blood-letting), soda and mineral water production, items for babies and invalids or the retail of groceries. Like any trade, entry into pharmacy could be achieved after serving an apprenticeship, and no particular qualifications were required.

The Pharmaceutical Society of Great Britain was founded in 1841 as a professional organisation to represent the interests of chemists and druggists, and promote pharmaceutical education as a specialist training with the aim of increasing professionalism and status. As J K Crellin points out in his article 'Pharmaceutical History and its Sources in the Wellcome Collections: The Growth of Professionalism in Nineteenth Century British Pharmacy' (*Medical History*, July 1967), the society wanted to make pharmacy 'a completely separate occupation from medicine' because only then could it be seen as a profession in its own right with a 'clear-cut, essential and socially important function'.

Although their roots in trade were a stigma, the main problem faced by pharmacists in their quest for professionalism and legal safeguards was the fact that anyone could call themselves a chemist and druggist. The

Pharmaceutical Journal of 1843–44 summed it up by saying: '… in most country towns not only is every Grocer and Oilman a Druggist, but almost every Druggist is a Grocer and Oilman. The Druggist has no badge or credentials to designate his superior qualification; in fact, he is not *of necessity* more qualified than the Grocer.'

At the forefront of the Pharmaceutical Society's educational work was its School of Pharmacy, opened in 1842, which quickly gained an excellent reputation for high-quality lectures and training. Two years later, for the first time in Britain, the school allowed its full-time students to supplement their chemistry lectures with practical work in its laboratory.

The society offered two types of examinations: minor (for the employed assistants of pharmacists) and major (for established pharmacists who were members of the society or who intended to join). Training at the School of Pharmacy for the society's examinations was much sought after, and many chemists and druggists referred to their studies there in advertisements and on business cards. This was despite the fact that such training was not necessary to enter pharmacy, since there were no compulsory entrance examinations until the 1868 Pharmacy Act was passed. The society also set up a museum and library, the weekly *Pharmaceutical Journal* and created opportunities for evening scientific meetings and research groups.

Legislation to safeguard the profession of chemists and druggists was slow to materialise. The Pharmacy Act of 1852 established the first statutory register of pharmacists, known as the *Register of Pharmaceutical Chemists*. However, it was not until 1868 that the Pharmacy Act set out minimum requirements for entry to the profession. The Act also made it compulsory for anyone involved in compounding and dispensing medicines, and selling certain scheduled poisons, to register with the Pharmaceutical Society, which could only be done after satisfying certain criteria.

From 1868, new entrants had to undergo an apprenticeship of several years with a practising pharmacist, after which they had to take a full- or part-time course of study. Only after this could candidates enter for the minor examination that was the new legal requirement. Those who were successful then had to register with the society, which published an annual *Register of Chemists and Druggists*. Employees who had qualified before 1868, and chemists and druggists who had been in business before this year, were automatically included on the register. A modified examination was available for pharmacy assistants who had been working for three years or more before 1868: this qualified them as a chemist and druggist. The major examination

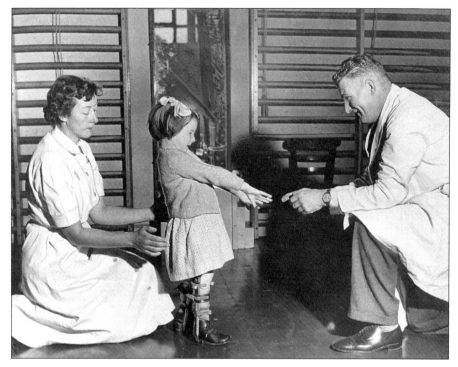

A physiotherapist helping a child in callipers to walk, 1930s. (Chartered Society of Physiotherapy, courtesy of the Wellcome Library, London)

was the advanced qualification for those who wanted to progress in the profession. Those who had passed this examination were included on the annual *Register of Pharmaceutical Chemists*, as well as the *Register of Chemists and Druggists*.

Physiotherapists

In the 1880s, massage had become recognised as a useful treatment for all manner of maladies. The voluntary hospitals started opening massage departments and employing 'massage nurses' specifically to carry out the work. These women were qualified nurses who chose to specialise in this area. As Jean Barclay points out in her book *In Good Hands*, at the same time, there were countless 'unqualified "rubbers", bath attendants, men who carried out a little electrical treatment after work and certain "masseuses" who have survived to this day by offering a lot more than massage'.

Private schools, offering training in massage and medical electricity, sprang up, initially in London, and then the provinces. Courses lasted between four and six months, and included lectures on anatomy and physiology as well as the practical aspects of massage.

A growing number of masseuses sought to distance themselves from these unqualified practitioners, and four nurses – Lucy Marianne Robinson, Rosalind Paget, Elizabeth Anne Manley and Margaret Dora Palmer – did so by founding the Society of Trained Masseuses in 1894. The setting-up of the society was partly an attempt to protect the profession's reputation after lurid reports of a series of sex scandals allegedly linked with masseuses appeared in the *British Medical Journal* in the summer of 1894.

The Society of Trained Masseuses was the first professional association for physiotherapists. It became the Incorporated Society of Trained Masseuses in 1900 and was renamed the Chartered Society of Massage and Medical Gymnastics in 1920. It assumed its current name, the Chartered Society of Physiotherapy (CSP), in 1944.

From the beginning, the society insisted on high standards from its members to ensure the good standing of the profession. The first rules stated that no massage was to be given without medical instruction, no advertising was allowed except in medical papers, no drugs could be sold to patients and 'no general massage for men to be undertaken but exceptions may be made for urgent and nursing cases at a doctor's special request'.

The society introduced a massage certificate which proved the recipient had been examined to a specified standard in massage techniques, elementary anatomy and 'the use of the Battery'. By 1914, 2,657 people had passed the society's exam in massage and 959 had opted to become members. Paid-up members of the society fell into two categories: ordinary members who had passed the massage exam and paid 5s. to join the Trained Nurses' Club; and associate members, who had been masseuses for years and were admitted without being examined for 10s. 6d.

At first, the society was dominated by women; male masseurs were not allowed to join the society until 1920. However, men such as asylum attendants and army orderlies could be examined for the massage certificate. In 1905, the society's high standards were recognised when the War Office asked it to examine a few of its army orderlies.

The society kept a register that helped put prospective employers in touch with masseuses. Members who found work through the register paid a percentage of their salary to the society – originally 10 per cent, but from 1899, the fees were adjusted according to a sliding scale from 5 per cent (on salaries of £3 or under) to 10 per cent.

As manipulative treatment was potentially dangerous if given incorrectly, masseuses and masseurs were at constant risk of being sued if they made a mistake. From the 1930s, the society offered comprehensive insurance schemes to cover their members from such risks.

In the First World War, massage was superseded by electrotherapy and hydrotherapy; manipulation was also popular. There was a constant need by the society's members to keep themselves educated and to undertake training in new areas of therapy. Radiography and occupational therapy both developed in the 1920s, as did remedial gymnastics in the 1940s; over the years, physiotherapy has co-existed with these other branches of the medical profession.

Psychiatrists

The organisation of psychiatry as a profession in Britain began in 1841 with the founding of the Association of Medical Officers of Asylums and Hospitals for the Insane. It was renamed the Medico-Psychological Association in 1865 and the Medico-Psychological Association of Great Britain and Ireland in 1887. After receiving a royal charter in 1926, it became the Royal Medico-Psychological Association (RMPA). Finally, in 1971 it changed its status to become the Royal College of Psychiatrists.

At first, the association was a means by which asylum superintendents could meet and communicate with their peers at annual conferences hosted at one another's asylums. This was important because working in a county asylum could be very isolating.

There were no additional medical qualifications required to be an asylum superintendent or to practise as a psychiatrist. In 1886, the Medico-Psychological Association introduced examinations for a Certificate in Psychological Medicine, which they administered. The examinations were held twice a year in England, Scotland and Ireland, and candidates had to be registered practitioners and at least 25 years old. In addition, they had to 'produce a certificate of having resided in an asylum (affording sufficient opportunity for the study of mental disorders) as clinical clerk or assistant medical officer for at least three months, or of having attended a course of lectures on insanity, and the practice of any asylum (where there is clinical teaching) for a like period.'

The new qualification was not compulsory, but by the 1890s facilities for the study of mental diseases had greatly increased. Provincial medical schools had lecturers on psychological medicine, with clinical instruction given in a nearby asylum. The Royal University of Ireland granted a diploma for the proficiency in the treatment of mental diseases to those who were graduates in medicine at the university.

Psychiatry was to prove immensely important when it came to treating shell-shocked soldiers during the First World War, and by the 1920s the Diploma in Psychological Medicine had been established.

Radiographers

When William Röntgen, the German physicist, discovered X-rays in November 1895, he not only found a medical innovation with huge potential for diagnostic use, he created a brand new field of medicine with opportunities for specialists and technicians: radiography. He had discovered that if he passed a high voltage through a vacuum tube, he could generate sufficient electromagnetic vibrations to penetrate the body and leave a photographic imprint on a plate on the other side. Röntgen demonstrated his technique on 22 December 1895 when he made a photograph of the bones in his wife's hand using these 'Röntgen rays' or X-rays.

For medicine, X-rays were invaluable in ruling out potential diagnoses where physical examination pointed to a number of possible diseases. Edward Shorter gives one example in 'Primary Care' in *The Cambridge Illustrated History of Medicine*. When percussion had indicated an area of dullness in the chest, an X-ray could determine if the problem was 'an aneurysm (or bulging) of the aorta – a typical late consequence of syphilis, a tumour or tuberculosis'. All three diseases create areas of dullness in the chest but the X-ray 'would show exactly what was at fault.'

X-ray equipment was introduced to Britain from 1896 onwards and was quickly implemented. Medical innovations meant nothing if hospitals could not afford to implement them. The apparatus was expensive and many hospitals relied on generous benefactors to provide it for them. However, it was vital to keep the appliances updated and train the technicians efficiently for quick and accurate diagnoses.

At this time, many large hospitals, including the London, were still lit by non-incandescent gas and did not have their own electrical supplies. This obviously had an impact on the practicalities of introducing and using X-ray equipment on a daily basis. Hospitals advertised for staff to run these new 'electrical departments', which were often combined with electro-therapeutic departments; they were usually managed by physicians or surgeons who already had a keen interest in photography.

In early 1896, Professor Arthur Schuster of Manchester University operated on a dancer's foot under X-ray, finding and extracting a needle from it. This was one of the first such operations using the new technology, perfectly demonstrating the potential of X-rays.

Early X-ray work was extremely hazardous because the danger of exposing hands to the unprotected X-ray tubes was not immediately recognised. At first, it was common for the X-ray operator to test the apparatus by looking at his own hand with a fluorescent screen. As a result, the first X-ray technicians suffered 'X-ray dermatitis'. These radiation injuries frequently led to carcinomas of the fingers, hands or arms, which could only be treated by amputating the affected limb. In many cases, the injuries were so serious it led to an early death.

In 1936, the German Röntgen Society erected a martyrs' memorial in the grounds of St George's Hospital, Hamburg, to commemorate the early pioneers of radiology who suffered radiation injuries or died as a result of their work. Fourteen British names were inscribed on the memorial, including Reginald Blackall, John Hall-Edwards and William Ironside Bruce. More British names were added in the 1950s.

The new profession of radiography sought to organise itself and raise its status. Medical practitioners, physicists and technicians founded the Röntgen Society in the same year. By 1902, many of the medical practitioners broke away and formed the British Electro-Therapeutic Society. As a parallel profession that was also using electrical therapy, it is not surprising that a large number of trained masseuses, who were members of the Chartered Society of Physiotherapists, studied for qualifications in X-ray technology at Guy's Hospital so that they could assist in this new work.

Doctors were in charge of most of the early X-ray work, but from around 1903 X-ray operators or assistants who were not medically trained were appointed to help with the workload. No special qualifications were required and they learnt their new skills on the job. As the importance of radiography became more widely recognised, increasing numbers of these X-ray assistants

JOHN F HALL-EDWARDS, SURGEON RADIOGRAPHER

Born in 1858, John Francis Hall-Edwards was a pioneer of X-ray technology in Birmingham. The *Medical Register* records that he became a licentiate of the Royal College of Physicians of Edinburgh in 1885 and set up a private practice in Moseley, near Birmingham. His hobby was photography and photo-micrography, and it was a natural step for him to take up radiography not long after Röntgen's discovery of X-rays. He quickly became known as an expert in this field and he was appointed radiographer to the General Hospital and the Royal Orthopaedic Hospital, both in Birmingham. He was also radiographer to the Birmingham Dental Hospital, the Birmingham and Midland Eye Hospital, and consulting radiographer to the Guest Hospital, Dudley.

On his appointment to the General, the *Nursing Record and Hospital World* reported that:

> In addition to the X-ray work, a photographic register of all important cases will be kept, a work for which Mr Hall-Edwards ... is specially qualified. A photographic laboratory, with the electrical apparatus necessary for work with the Röntgen rays, will be fitted up, and Mr Hall-Edwards, who has hitherto performed this work for the hospital at home, will attend at the hospital when required.

John's obituary in the *British Medical Journal* refers to his war record. Not surprisingly, radiographers were in great demand in times of war and after volunteering his services in the Boer War, he was appointed X-ray expert to the Imperial Yeomanry hospitals at Deelfontein and Pretoria. He was awarded the Queen's Medal with four clasps for his war work.

Not long after returning from South Africa, John began to suffer from the symptoms of X-ray dermatitis and was in pain for five years before having his left forearm and four fingers of the right hand amputated. As a result, he was granted a Civil List pension in 1908, but did not stop working. In 1914, despite his disabilities, he obtained a temporary commission as a major in the Royal Army Medical Corps. His tireless war work included acting as consulting radiographer to the First Southern and other military hospitals in the Birmingham area.

John continued to practise as a radiographer after the First World War, and died in 1926. His name is engraved on the martyrs' memorial in Hamburg.

were appointed. It became obvious that specialist training was needed, so new training courses were set up. The assistants became known as radiographers, and in 1920 twenty X-ray assistants who worked in the teaching hospitals of London founded the Society of Radiographers.

Anyone who had been actively and continually employed for ten years or more in the electro-therapeutic department or the X-ray department of a hospital or institution approved by the General Medical Council could apply to join. In 1921, the council developed a syllabus and introduced examinations for new members. In that year, there were 67 members, which rose to 164 by 1923.

During the Second World War, there was a shortage of radiographers, leading to an increase in their status and pay. Their importance to the war effort was reflected in the revised Schedule of Reserved Occupations of 1941 – male radiographers were allowed to serve in their own trade, and only those under the age of 25 could be called up.

Section 2
THE NURSING PROFESSION

Chapter 5
NURSING BEFORE 1860

In the eighteenth and nineteenth centuries, nursing was predominantly a female occupation, except in the army and lunatic asylums, where male orderlies did most of the nursing work.

Hospital nurses in the newly founded voluntary hospitals of the eighteenth century were untrained, usually illiterate and often coarse. Despite this apparent lack of skills, these nurses were drawn from the same social class as their patients, which meant that they could put them at ease and make them feel more at home in the strange environment of the hospital. Their experience of casualties of all kinds gained over the years was also extremely valuable, especially after the 1830s, when more critically injured patients started to be admitted to hospitals because of the increase in building work in developing towns and cities. John Delpratt-Harris, a consultant at the Royal Devon and Exeter Hospital, wrote in his book of the same name that the 'old-style' nurses were 'not above the ranks of those who became housekeepers and servants', and they 'could enter into the troubles of their patients and act as an intermediary.' Relationships between nurses and patients at this time were certainly on a more informal footing than later in the century, when trained nurses were introduced. It was common for the nurses to sleep close to the patients, either in an area of the ward which was partitioned off, or in cubicles between the wards. Nurses usually ate in the wards too. These old-style nurses continued to be employed in hospitals up until the last quarter of the nineteenth century.

In the early Victorian period, the duties of nurses were extremely limited, and were confined to changing beds, cleaning the wards and feeding patients, plus helping with dressings and applying poultices. As the 'pupil' system of assistants for the physicians and surgeons gradually died out, nurses took over the jobs they had undertaken. According to Ruth Hawker in her chapter 'For the Good of the Patient?' in *Nursing History: The State of the Art*, balneo-therapeutics (warm baths) were 'probably the first procedure for which nurses were seen to be important'. These baths, which were used to treat a wide range of conditions, were given jointly by nurses and pupils, and included hot, cold, sulphur and vapour baths.

Charles Dickens's alcoholic nurse Sairey Gamp in *Martin Chuzzlewit* is a stereotype, but it is hard to say how many early Victorian nurses matched it. Most were probably hard-working, but beer was certainly part of their daily allowance. On the occasion of Queen Victoria's Diamond Jubilee in 1897, the *British Medical Journal* published a retrospective article entitled 'Hospital Evolution in the Victorian Era'. In it, the writer referred to an old parliamentary report into the conditions of charitable hospitals in London in 1839. The report highlighted that in 1835 St Bartholomew's Hospital had twenty-nine sisters and seventy-five nurses. The nurses performed 'all the usual duties of servants, in waiting on and cleaning the patients, beds, furniture, wards, and stairs', indicating there was little time for actual nursing. This was before the separate class of ward maids was introduced to do the cleaning. These nurses were paid 7s. per week, and were entitled to two gowns and a cap each year. Their diet allowance was half a loaf and a pint of beer daily, 'with the meat from the hospital broth, also a dinner on Sunday'. Fifty of the nurses took it in turns to do night duty, and received 1s. 9d. a week extra for this work.

By 1860, the usual route into nursing in hospitals was still to be appointed as a 'scrubber' or ward maid, and to be promoted to a nurse after a period of good service. There was no system of training and little incentive towards career progression in terms of salary, accommodation or working conditions.

The first matrons

Until the 1870s, hospital matrons were efficient housekeepers whose main role was to supervise the domestic arrangements of the institution, such as managing the laundry, cooking and cleaning, as well as the staff who carried out these roles. Although managing the domestic affairs of a large hospital was a skilled job, the early matrons were not trained nurses. They appointed the nursing staff who worked in the hospitals, often in consultation with the medical staff, but they were not required to instruct them in their work.

Efficient matrons were invaluable to hospitals, since the daily laundry, cooking and cleaning had to run like clockwork to a defined routine. Less efficient matrons could tarnish a hospital's reputation if complaints from patients or staff were reported in the local press.

Christopher Maggs highlights the example of Anna Morrice in 'Profit and Loss and the Hospital Nurse', which appears in his book *Nursing History: The State of the Art*. Anna Morrice was the matron at the Royal South Hants

Infirmary and, between the years 1855 and 1861 her salary ranged from £41. 5s. 0d. to £48. 15s. 0d. In every year except the first, she successfully generated an income for the hospital in excess of her annual salary, simply by selling the kitchen waste or 'refuse'. In 1861, £59. 4s. 10d. was raised for the hospital in this way, more than covering the matron's own salary. This made her a very valuable employee.

Chapter 6

TRAINING AND QUALIFICATIONS

Florence Nightingale's training school for nurses

The reform of nursing started very slowly with Florence Nightingale establishing her training school at St Thomas's Hospital in 1860 under the Nightingale Fund. According to Monica Baly in 'The Nightingale Nurses: The Myth and the Reality', which appears in *Nursing History: The State of the Art*, Miss Nightingale was looking for a very specific type of woman. She believed that the kind of women most suited for the rigours of nursing had 'the morality and spiritual devotion of religious orders, the education of the middle-classes, combined with the hardiness of working-class girls'. Not surprisingly, this combination of qualities was difficult to find and the first trainees or 'probationers' came from the working classes.

Mrs Wardroper, the matron of St Thomas's Hospital, chose the first Nightingale probationers for the training course, which lasted a year. Probationers were paid £10 and were given rations of tea and sugar, washing and some outer clothing. A gratuity of £3 or £5 was also granted to them, depending on which class of award they had achieved after completing their training year and serving in a hospital for the sick poor.

Nurses had to be unmarried or widowed without dependent children. Miss Nightingale expected the recruits to be hard-working and did not believe a common day-room was necessary because it encouraged 'dawdling and gossiping'. Interestingly, the communal sitting-room was a feature of the majority of new nurses' homes that were built in the 1880s and 1890s.

The trained Nightingale nurses were known as 'sisters' and had to sign on for six years' service, a huge commitment when entering a profession that was not yet respectable or highly regarded. After the first year, the sisters could be sent anywhere in the country. Only at the end of the six-year period were the Nightingales able to apply for posts of their own choosing.

Rebecca Strong was a Nightingale-trained nurse who later became matron at Glasgow Royal Infirmary. In 'Nurses of Note', which appeared in the *British Journal of Nursing* in January 1924, she described her training at the end of the first year: 'You were supposed to have picked up enough knowledge and wisdom to fit you for pioneer work in other hospitals [and] you went wherever you were sent.' She added: 'Theoretical instruction was almost *nil*, which was a great disadvantage, the more enterprising had recourse to medical books ...' Rebecca Strong was sent first to Winchester for a year, followed by two years at Netley, before being appointed as matron at Glasgow.

The Nightingale probationers were assessed under fourteen sub-divisions, which give some indication of the type of work nurses were undertaking at the time:

1. Dressings
2. Applying Leeches
3. Enemas
4. Management of Trusses and Uterine Appliances
5. Rubbing
6. Helpless Patients
7. Bandaging
8. Making Beds
9. Waiting on Operations
10. Sick Cooking
11. Keeping Wards Fresh
12. Cleanliness of Utensils
13. Management of Convalescents
14. Observation of the Sick

In each of the sub-divisions, probationers were graded 'excellent', 'good', 'moderate', 'imperfect' or '0', and were also assessed on 'Punctuality, Quietness, Trustworthiness and Personal Neatness'. The last assessment was one of the probationer's moral character. A summary of Rebecca Strong's training report can be found in the appendix to Monica Baly's 'The Nightingale Nurses: The Myth and the Reality'. She was described as a 'good practical nurse'.

Although the Nightingale training system was by no means perfect, the sisters were employed throughout Britain and overseas in Australia, Canada, New Zealand and the United States, taking the Nightingale ideals with them. In British voluntary hospitals, Nightingale-trained nurses were highly sought after.

Lady probationers

From 1867, Miss Nightingale targeted better-educated lady recruits called 'special probationers'. The new 'specials', or 'lady probationers', paid for their board and lodging and were trained specifically to be superintendent nurses. They demanded higher-quality training because they were paying for it, and Mr John Croft was appointed to give lectures to them at St Thomas's.

By the 1880s, the idea of lady probationers had spread to most teaching hospitals. Such women were highly attractive to cash-strapped institutions, especially as they paid for their own training. The downside was that there was a distinct class difference between the new lady probationers and the ordinary probationers. In *The Hospitals 1800–1948*, Brian Abel-Smith points out that the lady probationers were people who had been 'head servants in gentlemen's families', 'widows in reduced circumstances' or 'persons who have lived in a respectable rank of life'.

The lady probationers expected a better standard of living accommodation than that provided for the ordinary nurses. This presented some financial difficulties to struggling voluntary hospitals because as the 'specials' were paying for their training, they could leave at any time if their demands were not met.

A career as a matron

For ambitious, trained nurses, working as a hospital matron offered a real career path in a respectable profession. Matronships across Britain were advertised in the local and national press, and applicants often had to be extremely mobile in their pursuit of the ideal post where they could make their mark. While some chose to stay at one hospital for twenty years or more, others moved regularly between hospitals.

The new matrons were no longer glorified housekeepers: they were educated, fully trained nurses. From the 1870s, the voluntary hospitals gradually replaced their old-style matrons with the new ones, sometimes called 'lady superintendents'. The new matrons were to have complete control over the nurses and female servants, in terms of recruiting, selecting and training them, as well as their working hours, living conditions and diet. Crucially, they were answerable only to the superintendent of the hospital, not the medical staff. Without doubt, the most important aspect of their role was to reform the nursing by devising an effective system of training. Many of the new matrons were Nightingale-trained, bringing the ideals and methods of that pioneering training system to their new posts.

EVA LÜCKES, MATRON OF THE LONDON

The daughter of a country gentleman, Eva Lückes epitomised the new class of women who were sought for the posts of lady superintendent and matron from the late 1870s onwards. She had been educated at a school in Malvern, then Cheltenham College, followed by a period on the Continent. On returning home to Gloucestershire after the death of her father, Eva spent time helping to run the house and visiting sick parishioners. She became interested in nursing as a career and joined the Middlesex Hospital as a lady probationer. After a few months, she was forced to give up this post because of ill-health, but later re-started and completed her training at the Westminster.

Eva Lückes, Matron at the London.
(The Windsor Magazine, 1900)

Once qualified, Eva became a night sister at the London for a few months, before being appointed as lady superintendent at the Pendlebury Children's Hospital in Manchester. In 1880, at the tender age of 24, Eva Lückes was appointed as matron of the London when it became vacant, despite many of the committee members believing she was 'much too young and pretty' to be a hospital matron.

According to A E Clark-Kennedy in *The London: A Study in the Voluntary Hospital System*, within twenty-four hours of taking up her duties at the London, Eva Lückes confronted the house committee, telling them that the London's nursing staff 'was grossly inadequate both in quality and numbers.' Her first recommendation was that 'lockers should be installed in the children's ward so that each one might have a separate towel and flannel instead of the same towel being used for all at the risk of spreading contagion.'

Eva Lückes remained as matron at the London until her death in 1919, radically reforming the nursing system there along the way.

Training for British nurses

By the 1880s, a variation of the probationer system of nurse training had been introduced into most large voluntary hospitals by the new matrons. Probationers were now a mixture of ordinary nurses, who were usually paid by the hospital during their training period, and lady probationers who paid for their own training.

As early as 1873, there was a nurses' training school at the London, introduced by the matron Miss Swift. She was not Nightingale-trained, but she took on many of the ideas from that system.

In Aberdeen in 1875, the Royal Infirmary set up the Donaldson Scheme, under which women trained for twelve months on the hospital's wards. The scheme was funded by the trustees of the late Robert Donaldson, who 'offered to grant a sum of money yearly to approved applicants who might … desire and agree to qualify themselves as Nurses.' Preference was given to applicants who were willing to undertake some of their training in the 'fever wards', which obviously could be a real risk to a nurse's health.

After twelve months, the nurses were given a Certificate of Efficiency and a monetary payment: 'the whole amount, including Dress, Lodging and Gratuity, not to exceed Fifteen Pounds to each Person.' The success of the scheme was such that the trained nurses were 'much valued and eagerly sought by professional men and private families'.

The effective training of nurses in both practical activities and theory became even more important with the introduction of antiseptic and aseptic techniques. It became clear that lectures should be a necessary part of nurses' training.

At first, Eva Lückes, the new matron at the London, gave lectures to the probationers herself; her first lecture was given on 30 June 1881. These lectures became standard reading when, three years later, they were published in her book *Lectures on General Nursing*. She also gave lectures to the sisters twice a year, and 'Hospital Sisters and their Duties' appeared in the second edition of her book, published in 1886.

However, more specialist knowledge was needed, and, after she persuaded them, the London's medical staff started to give lectures to the probationers on elementary anatomy and surgery, as well as physiology and medicine. Examinations were introduced from 1882 and certificates were awarded to successful candidates.

At Aberdeen's Royal Infirmary in 1886, a similar system of nurse training had been put into place by the matron Rachel Lumsden. By 1891, Aberdeen probationers had a three-year training programme. In Cardiff in 1888, the surgical and medical staff lectured to the nurses three times a week. According to the nursing committee minute book, their reading material for surgical lectures included:

I. Diagrams and Illustrations similar to those used by the St John's Ambulance Association
II. Lucker's Lectures on Nursing (a copy for each nurse) [this was probably Eva Lückes's manual]
III. Berkeley Hills 'Essentials of Bandaging'
IV. Blackie's Physiology
V. Hoblyns Dictionary of Medical Terms

Preliminary nurse training schools

Theoretical instruction was necessary to improve the nurses' training, but they had very little time away from the wards to make the most of the lectures. The answer lay in introducing preliminary training before starting the probationary period on the wards. The first preliminary training school for nurses in Britain was established at Glasgow in 1892, instigated by Rebecca Strong and the medical staff at the infirmary.

The idea of preliminary training took a while to be copied elsewhere in Britain. However, by June 1895, the London had its own preliminary training school at Tredegar House. Even after the nurses started as true probationers, they were given off-duty time for study, lectures and classes.

An unidentified Victorian nurse, c.1885. (Author's collection)

87 LORD ST.
LIVERPOOL.

Career structure

Along with teaching, nursing offered Victorian middle-class women a career in a respectable occupation. From the 1880s, the number of female British nurses rose steadily and there was a defined career structure for nurses, which was similar across Britain, based on the principles of training set out by Florence Nightingale.

Like other city hospitals, Birmingham's General sought to review and formalise its nursing arrangements as a result of an ever-increasing number of in- and out-patients. In 1884, it stated that nurses during their first year of training be called probationers, afterwards as staff nurses. The term 'staff nurse' was normally used to describe someone who had finished their three years of probationer training, so Birmingham's terminology may not be the same as elsewhere. At Birmingham, certificates of training were given after not less than three years' service. Head nurses were promoted from the staff nurses 'and not obtained from other Hospitals'. Above the head nurses were superintendent nurses, who were answerable to the matron.

At the time, the General had a total of fifty nurses on its staff: three superintendent nurses, fourteen head nurses, twenty-nine staff nurses and five probationers. The head nurses were later known as 'charge nurses'. By 1892, the number of nurses had increased to sixty-six, including superintendents, theatre, masseuse and surgery nurses, 'this number being still below the average of many large Hospitals'.

By the 1890s, nurses were being appointed in hospitals to carry out specific functions. Training was on-the-job, but nurses who chose to specialise in this way were in demand. They included theatre nurses accustomed to the use of chloroform and ether as anaesthetics, and massage nurses (also known as masseuses or rubbers), who were in short supply in the new electrical departments. Massage and electrical therapy had been found to be of great benefit to patients with painful joint conditions, which could be treated with multiple out-patient appointments. For example, at the London in 1904, there were 13,000 attendances of out-patients for massage treatment.

Towards registration

A significant section of the matrons and lady superintendents wanted to raise the status of nursing through registration. For this reason, the British Nurses' Association was established in 1887 by Mrs Bedford Fenwick, who, before her marriage, was Ethel Gordon Manson. She had been appointed matron of St Bartholomew's at the early age of 24, but left her post six years later to marry.

The aim of the association was to obtain full professional status for nursing by registering qualified nurses, with an emphasis on uniforms and adequate training. Opponents of registration – including Florence Nightingale, Eva Lückes and some sections of the medical profession – feared it would limit the number of probationers.

Campaigning for state registration continued throughout the 1890s, but factions within the profession could not agree about its purpose and how it should be done. The Midwives Registration Act of 1902 achieved state registration for midwives – this had also been a long, slow process. A House of Commons Select Committee was set up in 1904 to consider the issue of state registration for nurses, but no action was taken by the government after the resulting report was presented, even though it was positive about registration.

Various Private Member's Bills were introduced over the next decade, but did not garner sufficient support from Parliament. Although the valuable contribution made by nurses during the First World War did not go unnoticed, the use of partially trained and untrained women as nurses in Voluntary Aid Detachments (VADs) was seen as a threat to trained nurses. Efforts were subsequently renewed to bring about state registration. A turning point came in 1916, when the College of Nursing, which later became the Royal College of Nursing, was set up. Three years later, another Private Members' Bill was put through Parliament, and separate Nurses Registration Acts were finally passed for England/Wales, Scotland and Ireland in December 1919.

The Nurses Registration Act 1919

The new legislation established the General Nursing Council, which was responsible for setting up a register of nurses, examining them, and approving training schools to provide high-quality courses. The register was to have a main section for general nurses, and supplementary sections for male nurses, mental nurses, fever nurses and sick children's nurses. There was no provision for nurses with a lower standard of training.

From 1941, the Ministry of Health guaranteed cash salaries for student nurses, and hospitals were encouraged to pay nurses a minimum wage. In the same year, the Royal College of Nursing set up a committee to look into and define the role of assistant nurses. The result was the 1943 Nurses Act which established the Roll of Assistant Nurses, together with a two-year training requirement. Again, the General Nursing Council was responsible for the roll, setting the syllabus for the examinations, and approving the training schools.

Chapter 7

WORKING CONDITIONS FOR NURSES

In the Victorian era, nursing was reformed and developed as a respectable profession for middle-class women and girls. However, it was also an extremely strenuous occupation and hours were long. Before the separate class of scrubbers and washermaids was introduced, nurses were expected to do the scrubbing and cleaning of the wards as well as the nursing.

Typical working hours can be seen at the London. In the late 1880s, day nurses worked fourteen hours with two hours off, while the night nurses worked twelve. Days off were rare, although there was a fortnight's annual holiday. By 1905, the nurses were allowed three hours off duty during the day and a whole day off once a fortnight.

In the 1880s, most large voluntary hospitals had similar nursing arrangements to that of the Glasgow Royal Infirmary. It had sixty-two nurses for thirty-one wards, divided into day and night nurses, with one of each for

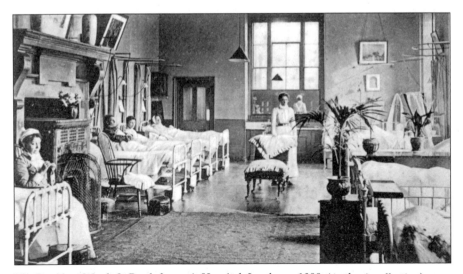

The President Ward, St Bartholomew's Hospital, London, c.1900. (Author's collection)

every ward. There were also twenty-nine probationers who were used as a kind of 'floating staff'. One probationer was assigned to each ward as an assistant, but the most experienced were 'selected to do duty for the regular nurses when on leave of absence or disabled by sickness'. The nurses were assisted by twenty scrubbers and cleaners, and sixteen washerwomen and laundrymaids.

Health

A large supply of probationers was needed because the nursing profession was made up of young women who could not continue their careers if they chose to marry. Good health was essential at the start of probationer training because nursing was so physically demanding, but finding suitable applicants of sufficient fitness and with the right attitude was often a hit-and-miss affair.

The London tried to limit the number of 'false starts'. It did not accept any probationers for training unless they had been interviewed and passed a medical examination. New probationers were not allowed to sign a contract with the hospital until they had completed a month's trial. By contrast, in 1905, the matron of Glasgow's Royal Infirmary never interviewed the candidates beforehand and rarely took up references.

At Birmingham's General Hospital in the 1890s, the nursing committee specified a minimum height of 5 feet 2 inches and 8 stone in weight for probationers to ensure they were strong enough for the work. However, few applicants matched this specific criteria, and by 1900, the minimum weight was withdrawn. It was also considered that women between 23 and 35 were the most suitable age for nursing.

Living quarters

Before the 1890s, living accommodation for nurses left a lot to be desired. In many hospitals, they slept in areas between the wards that were partitioned off, and were therefore cramped and insanitary. A visitor to Birmingham's General Hospital in 1877 recorded his impressions of the nurses' accommodation:

> I have visited for the first time the nurses' bed-rooms or rather stalls for sleeping in, and am surprised at the nature of the accommodation provided. It appears to me altogether unfit for the purpose, more

especially when the trying nature of a nurse's duties are considered – I respectfully suggest that sleeping accommodation for hospital nurses should be outside of the hospital.

The house committee promptly rejected the suggestion.

Many hospitals adapted existing properties which were unsuitable, rather than providing a purpose-built nurses' home. It was not until the late 1890s that most hospitals had their own nurses' home separate from the hospital, largely because the increasing numbers of nurses required on the staff forced their hand. The new accommodation usually included a dining-room, separate bedrooms for the nurses, and a communal living-room with easy chairs, books, and often a piano. Many nurses' homes were built to coincide with Queen Victoria's Golden and Diamond Jubilees in 1887 and 1897.

Pay

Nurses' pay varied across Britain, though in all hospitals the salaries of probationers was low because they were, in effect, undertaking a kind of apprenticeship for which they were being trained. Incremental increases were offered up to a specified maximum, in order to try to retain staff.

In 1905, the secretary, steward and matron's assistant of the London visited Glasgow Royal Infirmary, Glasgow Western Infirmary, Edinburgh's Royal Infirmary, the Leeds General Infirmary and Birmingham's General Hospital. The visits were primarily to ascertain how the hospitals were able to run at a lower annual cost than at the London, but their observations touched on all aspects of hospital life, including the salaries of nurses.

At Glasgow's Western Infirmary, probationers signed for four years with no preliminary training. They received £10 for the first year, £15 in the second and third years, and £25 in the fourth year. Nurses were paid £30 a year while sisters received £30 a year, rising by £2 a year to a maximum of £40.

At the London, probationers were paid £12 in the first year, £20 for the second and £24 in the third year. Nurses received between £24 and £27 per annum, while sisters were paid between £30 and £40.

Edinburgh's Royal Infirmary was less generous to its probationers. They received just £8 for the first year, £12 in the second and £20 in the third. Nurses were paid £25 a year and sisters received £30, rising by £2 a year to a maximum of £40.

In Leeds, the General Infirmary paid its probationers £10 in the first year, £14 in the second and £18 for the third. Staff nurses were paid £30 per annum, and sisters received £35 for two years, and then £40.

At Birmingham, no salary at all was paid to probationers in the first year, presumably to discourage time-wasters from applying. They also had to pay a premium of 20 guineas if they only signed on for three years; no fee was charged if they signed for four. No figures were given for nursing salaries in the 1905 report, but in 1892, probationers in the second year received £16, and £18 in the third, increasing by £2 per annum after that to a maximum of £24.

The length of training for probationers was not uniform across the country, with some hospitals only providing two-year courses, and others up to four. By the early twentieth century, three years became the standard course length: this was seen as a minimum to train a nurse properly to carry out her duties effectively and professionally.

By the late nineteenth and early twentieth century, nursing had become a viable profession for middle-class women and girls. Charles Booth in his *Life and Labour in London* cited a number of advantages of nursing as a profession, including the fact that '… the earnings of the nurse compare favourably with those of the daily governess and the upper domestic servant, while her social rank is distinctly superior to that of the latter.' He also believed that 'The prospects of marriage are … better, because of the constant contact into which she is brought with the students and their teachers in the course of her duties.'

Diet

Although nursing was physically demanding, at first, hospitals did not provide regular meals for their nurses, or breaks in which to eat them. In the 1860s, the nurses at Glasgow Royal Infirmary were provided with rations which they had to cook in their wards. According to an annual report from 1880, the diet was so meagre that the nurses 'were under great temptation … of adding to their own scanty fare from the diet supplied for the patients.' Nurses were not allowed to take food from a patient, even if it was offered, and, if caught, they could face dismissal for flouting the rules. This was a common rule in most hospitals. By 1892, three meals a day were provided for the Glasgow nurses.

At the London, breakfast was not provided for the day or night staff before going on duty, and nurses had to eat their rations when and where they could. After 1880, the situation improved significantly as breakfast, dinner and supper were provided in the dining-room for everyone.

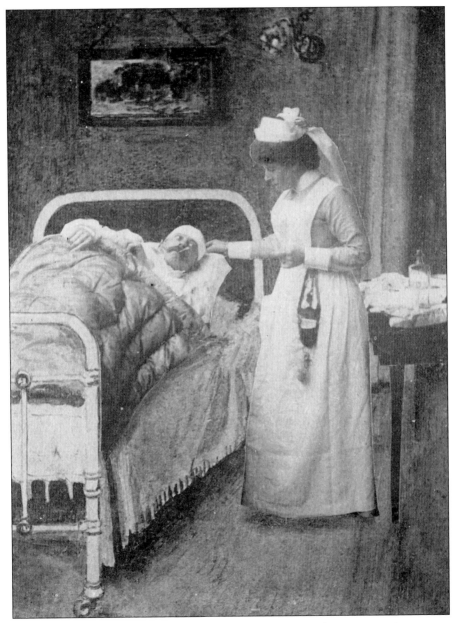

'The Nurse and her Patient: Taking the Temperature', c.1900. (Author's collection)

Dismissals and resignations

Like the other staff (and the patients), nurses were bound by the strict rules of the hospitals in which they worked. Flouting one of the many rules could lead to dismissal, which might have an impact on a nurse's future employment in another hospital. It was forbidden, for example, to accept gifts or money from patients or their relatives, and to fraternise with medical students in or outside the hospital.

Insobriety, poor health and unsuitability for the work were the main reasons for dismissals of hospital nurses. In Glasgow in 1880, 30-year-old Annie Padley managed just seven months of training as a probationer. Although she left of her own accord, the register notes that she was 'unsuitable' and in the character column it is recorded that she was 'a flirt'. At some point, Annie must have returned to the hospital and been re-admitted as a probationer. On the 1881 census, she is recorded at the Glasgow Royal as a hospital nurse. Another nurse who was asked to leave Glasgow in 1880 was dismissed because of her 'Abuse of Chloroform'. Her character was 'good, otherwise'.

Ellen Chapman, 23 at the time, started as a probationer at Birmingham's General Hospital in April 1898 and had passed two assessments in May and August, but left on 15 September. The reason given was that she had been 'Found asleep on night duty in charge of special cases (twice)'.

Even highly regarded nurses could be dismissed for neglect of duty. Alice Paget had been admitted on trial at Birmingham's General Hospital in November 1887 and promoted to staff nurse a month later. By March 1890, she was a charge nurse and received a medal in February 1892. The nursing committee minute book stated that medals were 'to be reserved as special rewards (say after 5 years)'. However, on 25 November 1892, Alice was dismissed by the house committee. The minute book recorded that 'it is the painful duty ... to discharge Nurse Paget and to suspend her from duty at once.'

No further reason is given for Alice's dismissal but the previous minute provides a clue: 'The House Governor reported that Albert Riddle aged 11 had run away on November 21st last from Ward 22.' It appears likely that Alice Paget's dismissal was linked with Albert's escape from the hospital.

Registers of staff reveal three main reasons that nurses resigned of their own accord: their inability to cope with the work, leaving for a promotion at another hospital or leaving to get married. This last scenario was the reason for needing large numbers of probationers to come through the training system – when a nurse married, she was unable to continue in her occupation because most hospitals stipulated that their nurses be single or widowed without dependent children. There were rare exceptions to this rule. For instance, Rebecca Strong, a Nightingale nurse, and later matron at the Glasgow Royal Infirmary, was widowed with a young child. She was able to pursue a career in nursing because she was able to show that her daughter was being looked after by relatives.

Long-serving nurses

Despite the hardships of the job, there were a few long-serving nurses in most hospitals. The Glasgow Royal Infirmary's register of nurses reveals that Kate Bell, a nurse at the hospital, left on 21 March 1916, having died after forty-nine years' service. She was then aged 73 and had been working continuously up to within a few weeks of her death. According to the *British Journal of Nursing*, it was she who was 'the trusted nurse who made the antiseptic when Lord Lister was evolving his treatment'. Kate did not live to enjoy retirement, but by the 1880s, long-serving nurses were often entitled to pensions at the discretion of the hospital.

At Birmingham's General Hospital in 1883, the house committee reported that 'Phoebe Taylor, the head nurse in Wards 22 & 23 was no longer capable, on account of years and diminished activity, efficiently to discharge her duties.' Three months later, another minute stated that 'Phoebe Taylor, the Head Nurse of the Burns Ward, be relieved from further duty and a pension of 7s/- a week be paid to her.' Born in Leicestershire, Phoebe was by now 60 years of age.

This pension of 7s. a week seems to have been standard for some time, as the following year, 'Nurse Elizabeth Lowe of Ward 6 on account of good service to the Hospital for twenty-eight years' was awarded the same amount.

ELIZABETH MARY REED, PROBATIONER TO QUEEN'S NURSE

Born in 1889 in St Stythians, Cornwall, and educated in Redruth and Truro, Elizabeth Mary Reed was in teaching before she entered the nursing profession. At the age of 21, she started her probationer training at the Guest Hospital in Dudley, where she was sent by the Nursing Institute, Worcester. The *Register of Nurses and Servants* states that the institute paid a premium of 10 guineas for her training.

The *Nurses' Probationers Register* for the Guest Hospital reveals that Elizabeth started her training on 17 September 1910. It records the number of weeks she spent in each ward, whether she was on day or night duty, when she took her holidays and when she passed each of her three examinations. This gives a good indication of the structure of probationers' training at this time. Perhaps of most interest are the comments recorded in the columns for the sister's report as to Elizabeth's work in their wards and the matron's report as to conduct, tidiness, etc. Adverse comments could significantly affect the chances of a probationer passing her training, although it is possible they could have been as a result of personality clashes between the probationer and ward sister, or even the matron.

The matron's first comments about Elizabeth note that she is 'Bright & intelligent but manners want to be quieter'. Until October 1911, the sisters' opinions of Elizabeth's work were that she was doing well and that her conduct was good. After a three-week stint of night duty in Ward 1 (Victoria), the night sister wrote that her 'Conduct might be more satisfactory.' In December 1911, the matron noted that Elizabeth's conduct was 'not satisfactory, is not truthful'. No further details are given about the incident(s) which caused this comment, but it was not serious enough to halt her training. After this time, the comments improve, with the ward sisters mostly recording that Elizabeth's work and conduct were very good. Even the matron wrote that her conduct was 'good' or 'very good', but she continued to write from time to time that Elizabeth 'ought to be quieter.'

Towards the end of her training, Elizabeth had the chance to prove herself as she was given the task of being the sister's locum in the Victoria Ward for three weeks (probably while the sister was on holiday). She does not appear to have had any problems with this as the comments

Entry for Elizabeth Mary Reed in the Guest Hospital Probationer Register, 1910–13. (Courtesy of Dudley Archives and Local History Service)

state: 'Has done well as Sister's Locum in Victoria. Work & conduct very good.'

Elizabeth left the Guest Hospital on 27 September 1913, having completed her training. Her overall conduct was recorded at the bottom of the register page as 'good'. This does not match up with the final verdict given in the *Register of Nurses and Servants*, which notes that Elizabeth left at the end of her training and her conduct was 'not altogether satisfactory'.

Despite these dubious closing remarks about her conduct, Elizabeth returned to Worcester for the next stage of her nursing career. Instead of applying to another hospital as a staff nurse, she immediately started six months of 'district training'. This training was designed to equip her to become a 'Queen's Nurse'. The Queen's Nursing Institute was set up in 1889 to provide training for district nurses. Elizabeth appears on the *Queen's Nurses Roll* as No. 4846. The roll records the nature of the district training she received in Worcester. She attended lectures in 'Hygiene, Physiology & Chemistry of Daily Life, Tuberculosis, and Midwifery'. Prior to this, she had no midwifery training. After completing the six-month course, Elizabeth sat the roll examination, in which she achieved 43½ marks out of a possible 60.

Elizabeth was placed on the *Queen's Nurses Roll* on 1 April 1914 and worked as a 'daily visiting nurse' in Worcester. The first annual inspection in March 1915 records that she was a 'very good nurse … has initiative; is quick & capable'. A year later, the second inspection notes that she was a 'Quick & capable worker, pleasant manner, & inspires confidence, much liked'. It would appear that Elizabeth was better suited to working as a district nurse than to hospital nursing; although the superintendent reported that she was 'A kind nurse. Much liked by her patients', she might 'Do better in a Home for a time'.

By May 1914, Elizabeth had received a Bronze Badge in recognition of her service with the Queen's Nursing Institute. This is recorded in the *Badge Register*.

The *Queen's Nurses Roll* has a lengthy document for each nurse recorded in it, with a wealth of valuable information for the family historian. There is a useful column for 'Other Qualifications & Remarks'. This states that Elizabeth was a cyclist (an essential attribute of a district nurse at that time) and that in 1915 she was the sister of a VAD hospital, taking classes for the VADs.

The document records that Elizabeth left Worcester on 20 September 1916 to work for JFNS, which was probably another district nursing association.

On 26 March 1918, Elizabeth resigned from the Queen's Nursing Institute 'to be married'. The final report states that she was 'A quick and capable worker, inspiring confidence. Conduct very good'.

Chapter 8

PLACES OF WORK

A lthough it might be assumed that hospitals were the main place of work for nurses, in the Victorian and Edwardian period this was not the case. Steven Cherry notes in *Medical Services and the Hospitals in Britain 1860–1939* that in 1881, there were 35,216 female nurses in Britain. The numbers had risen to 53,003 by 1891, and 64,209 by 1901. In total, there were 69,200 nurses of both sexes, but of this figure only 12,500 were trained or registered.

This meant a very high proportion of those calling themselves 'nurses' were either probationers in training, acting as 'wet' nurses or 'monthly' nurses, or nursing in a more informal capacity. In 1901, fewer than a third of nurses worked in hospitals and most of the remainder were nursing privately. By 1931, there were 153,670 nurses of both sexes, but only 50,000 were trained or registered. Private nursing, working in a Poor Law institution or lunatic asylum, or in the British Army or Royal Navy were all additional places of work nurses could consider, aside from hospitals. The work of mental nurses in asylums is described in Chapter 9, 'Development of the Nursing Profession'.

Private nursing

There were two ways a nurse could work in the private sector: either by being sent by the hospital or agency for which she worked, or on a self-employed basis by advertising her services. It was, however, in the nurse's interests to be hospital-trained since the upper and middle classes sought nurses of the highest calibre.

'Monthly' nurses were self-employed and, although their title refers to their usual role of looking after a mother and baby in the month after childbirth, she might also have been employed to nurse the elderly or other private patients. Midwives could also be self-employed.

There was an insatiable demand for private hospital-trained nurses to attend upper- and middle-class patients in their own homes. Charitable voluntary hospitals, always trying to balance the books, were quick to take advantage of this new way to generate extra income. The hospitals sent their

A private nurse with an elderly patient, c.1905. (Author's collection)

nurses out to the patients' homes, and they usually returned to the institution at night. Patients could either request care per day, or continuous night nursing, for which different rates were charged. At the Cardiff Royal Infirmary, the fees in 1888 for continuous night nursing were 30s. per week and 35s. to non-subscribers.

Poor Law nursing

The other major institution employing nurses was the workhouse (or poorhouse in Scotland). Nurses in Poor Law institutions were subject to the orders of the master, matron and medical officer, as well as the conditions set by the unions that ran the workhouses. Many unions, mindful of the financial burden on the ratepayers, resisted appointing paid nurses until compelled to do so.

The salaries of paid workhouse nurses varied between £12 and £50 per annum, plus board and an allowance of beer or porter. They were required to supervise the unpaid paupers who did most of the nursing. After the reform of workhouse infirmaries in the 1860s, there were slight increases in the number of paid workhouse nurses. However, the use of paupers as nurses was not banned until after 1897, and only then was there a significant rise in the number of paid appointments.

It was rare for paid workhouse nurses to be hospital-trained simply because the voluntary hospitals offered higher salaries, better working conditions, higher-quality training and superior accommodation.

Although the Scottish Poor Law authorities had introduced the first national nurse-training system in 1885, English and Welsh Poor Law infirmaries were slow to follow suit. The *Lancet* surveyed fifty English Poor Law infirmaries in the 1890s and only four had 'nursing arrangements comparable with voluntary hospitals'.

From the 1870s, the Poor Law Board introduced a scheme which encouraged larger workhouse infirmaries to train nurses by appointing probationers; the medical officer and head nurse would provide the year's training. Towards the end of the nineteenth century, both the training and accommodation for workhouse nurses started to improve. By 1897, all Poor Law infirmaries with three or more nurses had to employ a superintendent nurse, who could only be trained by an infirmary with a resident doctor.

The British Army

From the 1860s, the British Army offered another career path to nurses, with the attraction of overseas travel and a pension as reward for long service.

During the Crimean War (1854–56), Florence Nightingale took thirty-eight women with her to Scutari Hospital to help tend the wounds of the neglected, injured soldiers. This introduction of female nursing into army hospitals helped to improve the rate of recovery and prevented many avoidable deaths through better sanitation and diet.

After the war, the importance of proper training for army nurses and surgeons was keenly felt. The Royal Victoria Military Hospital at Netley near Southampton was built as a direct result of the experiences of the Crimean War; the foundation stone was laid in May 1856. While Netley was being built, the garrison hospital at Woolwich was converted in 1861. Netley finally opened in 1863, and was specifically designed to train army nurses and doctors, and to treat sick and wounded soldiers effectively so they could be returned to duty as soon as possible. Netley's close proximity to the port of Southampton meant that hospital ships could easily dock and disembark their patients. From 1900, ambulance trains on the new railway line were used to transport the patients from Southampton to Netley.

At the time, the Royal Victoria was the largest British military hospital, with around 1,000 beds spread across 138 different wards. With such large numbers of patients, an efficient nursing staff was essential and Florence Nightingale provided input and advice about how best to implement this. New regulations for general military hospitals came into force in August 1861. They recommended that male Army Hospital Corps orderlies be employed (one to every ten sick), and that a minimum female staff should include a superintendent, four nurses, and one linen nurse. Cases were to be split between medical, surgical and venereal wards, and no female nurses were allowed to work in the latter.

The first 'superintendent general of female nurses' at Netley was Jane Catherine Shaw Stewart, who had been a nursing sister during the Crimean War. She was the first woman to appear on the *Army List*, although she was non-commissioned. It was she who inaugurated the female army nursing service when she set up a staff of six nurses at the newly built Royal Herbert Hospital in Woolwich. At Netley, she was assisted by five nurses.

Jane Stewart's successor was Jane Deeble, who arrived in 1869, bringing with her six Nightingale nurses from St Thomas's Hospital. The training the nurses received prior to their arrival was completely inadequate for the work at Netley. As Anne Summers notes in *Angels and Citizens: British Women as Military Nurses 1854–1914*, 'in the first month, one sister nearly poisoned a patient by dosing him with liniment instead of cod liver oil.'

By 1881, the Army Nursing Service had been founded, and two years later every military hospital with 100 beds or more had a staff of sisters. Their uniforms consisted of grey ward dresses and scarlet red capes. The nurses

HELEN CAMPBELL NORMAN, RRC

Miss Helen Campbell Norman, lady superintendent of the Army Nursing Service, on board the hospital ship Trojan. (*Illustrated London News*, 28 October 1899)

Born in Peshawar, India, in 1856, Helen Campbell Norman was the second daughter of a lieutenant colonel in the Indian Army. Military life was in her blood, and in September 1882, after training as a nurse at St Mary's Hospital in Paddington, she went to Egypt during the war as a nursing sister. When she returned to England in May 1883, Helen was awarded the Royal Red Cross in recognition of her nursing services.

In October that year, she joined the Army Nursing Service and two years later she served for three months at the base hospital in Suakim and afterwards on the hospital ship *Ganges*. For this work, Helen was given the Egyptian Medal and clasp for Suakim, as well as the Khedive's Star. After returning to Netley, she was sent to Devonport and then to the military hospital in Gibraltar, where she acted as superintendent of nurses.

This was to equip her for the role of lady superintendent of the Army Nursing Service based at the Royal Victoria Hospital, Netley – a post which she held from 1889 until 1902. Helen also served during the Boer War, and the *Illustrated London News* reported in October 1899 that she had arrived in South Africa aboard the hospital ship *Trojan*.

In February 1902, the *Nursing Record and Hospital World* reported that 'Miss Norman ... has been ordered complete rest for six months and will be leaving Netley at the end of the week.' Helen died in Gunnar, Tenerife in August 1913, aged 57.

were soon demonstrating their capabilities in the Zulu War (1879–80), the Egyptian Campaign (1882) and the Sudan (1883–85).

In 1893, when Helen Campbell Norman, the lady superintendent of the Army Nursing Service, was interviewed at Netley by the *Nursing Record*, she commented on how the nurses and male orderlies worked together: 'Intelligent and capable men are enlisted, and some are chosen from the ranks of the army to be specially trained to perform many of those offices for the sick which in an ordinary Hospital are delegated to the Nurses. Here, the ... Nursing Sisters have control over these men; each lady having under her special care and superintendence about eight wards'.

At that time, the headquarters for the army nurses was at Netley and, by then, no nurse could enter the Army Nursing Service without first completing three years' training in a general hospital. Nurses could be drafted at any time to undertake service overseas.

Princess Christian's Army Nursing Service Reserve (PANSR)

Princess Christian was Queen Victoria's third daughter and she became interested in military nursing. The Princess Christian's Army Nursing Reserve was formed in 1897, made up of trained and experienced nurses. It was not long before the reserve was needed and they served with distinction during the Boer War. By 1907, the reserve was disbanded and members joined the QAIMNS.

Queen Alexandra's Imperial Military Nursing Service (QAIMNS)

In 1902, Queen Alexandra's Imperial Military Nursing Service replaced the Army Nursing Service (ANS) and the Indian Nursing Service (INS) by royal warrant. The Indian Nursing Service section was called Queen Alexandra's Imperial Military Nursing Service for India until 1926, when 'for India' was removed from the title.

When war broke out in 1914, there were fewer than 300 QAIMNS nurses – by 1918, numbers had increased to more than 10,000 (along with members of the QAIMNS Reserve). Military nurses served alongside the British Army during the First World War on hospital ships, as well as in France, the Balkans, the Middle East and the Mediterranean.

In 1926, the nursing sisters of the QAIMNS were granted regular army officer rank, but they had to wait until 1941 for an army commission and rank structure. During the Second World War, QAIMNS nurses served in the Far East, South Africa, Greece, Norway and Iceland. By now, their uniforms had changed to battledress blouses and khaki trousers. After the war, in 1949, the QAIMNS became a corps of the British Army and was renamed the Queen Alexandra's Royal Army Nursing Corps.

Voluntary Aid Detachments (VADs)

The Voluntary Aid Detachments were started by the Red Cross and St John's Ambulance Service in 1909 to assist the army medical service. Members (known simply as VADs) could be male or female, but the most well known were the nursing volunteers who were trained in first aid and basic nursing skills; they were usually upper- and middle-class women.

The important thing to realise if your ancestor was a VAD is that she was not a qualified nurse. She would have been involved in administering first aid, cooking and cleaning. Many VADs served overseas, and the minimum age for this was 23. Some VADs later qualified as nurses in peacetime. VADs were also used in a similar way during the Second World War, although by then they came under the army's jurisdiction, even though they were civilian volunteers.

The Royal Navy

For a long time, nursing in the Royal Navy was of a very low standard. Sick and injured sailors were left in taverns or lodgings at the next port of call, tended by a local surgeon, and nursed by whoever was available. Conditions were little better at Haslar, the first purpose-built naval hospital, where the nursing was carried out by the widows of sailors and marines or by old pensioners.

During the Crimean War, Eliza Mackenzie took a party of six experienced nurses to Therapia, Constantinople, where the navy had its base hospital. Like Florence Nightingale, Eliza and her nurses improved conditions at the hospital and helped to save the lives of many injured or sick patients. Unlike Florence Nightingale, her efforts did not bring about an immediate change in the naval nursing system. It was another thirty years before it was recommended that a similar system to the Army Nursing Service be put into place for the Royal Navy.

In 1884, the first trained naval nursing sisters were appointed to the Naval Nursing Service at Haslar and Plymouth. One of their main responsibilities was to instruct the newly formed male 'sick berth staff' in practical nursing. In 1902, the Naval Nursing Service became known as Queen Alexandra's Royal Naval Nursing Service (QARNNS).

By 1910, civilian hospitals were forming large numbers of reserve staff in case war broke out, and the QARNNS Reserve did the same. Both male and female VADs assisted the nursing staff of the QARNNS during the First and Second World Wars. After the war, in 1949, the Women's Royal Naval Service (WRNS) founded a medical branch, and WRNS 'sick berth attendants' started to be trained.

Royal Air Force Nursing Service

The Royal Air Force Nursing Service (RAFNS) was founded in June 1918, and became a permanent branch of the RAF by 1921. Two years later, it was renamed Princess Mary's Royal Air Force Nursing Service (PMRAFNS).

At first, the nurses looked after patients in rehabilitation hospitals, station medical centres and other military hospitals, in Britain and overseas. During the Second World War, their main responsibility was to tend patients before they were evacuated from the war zone. Later, in-flight nursing skills became a major part of their role.

Chapter 9

DEVELOPMENT OF THE NURSING PROFESSION

Midwives

From time immemorial, the 'local woman' or midwife helped the women in her community to give birth. She was not formally trained, although some midwives had undergone a form of apprenticeship. Many were widows, since it was not thought appropriate for unmarried women to be involved with childbirth.

From Tudor times, the Church of England licensed midwives to enable them to baptise newborn babies in the absence of an ordained clergyman. These women were licensed by the bishop of the diocese in which they worked, and were required to subscribe to the Thirty-Nine Articles of Religion, proving they were part of the Church of England. The midwives swore to be 'diligent, faithful and ready to help every woman travailing of child, the poor as well as the rich; not to forsake the poor woman and leave her to go to the rich, nor to exercise any manner of witchcraft, charms, sorcery or invocation'.

The licensing of midwives died out in the eighteenth century, at about the same time as man-midwives, or *accoucheurs*, became more common. As Joan Lane points out in *A Social History of Medicine*, it was generally considered that 'a midwife's task was to deliver a live child, while a male practitioner was sought in a crisis to deliver a dead one.'

In the last quarter of the nineteenth century, it was still the case that any woman could call herself a midwife and charge for her services because no training or qualifications were required. While many such women were highly experienced, others knew little of the importance of hygiene in childbirth, or had any knowledge of anatomy. This left the poorest in society, who could not afford the fee charged by a qualified doctor, at the mercy of these unqualified women.

According to Steven Cherry in *Medical Services and the Hospitals in Britain 1860–1939*, midwives attended around 70 per cent of births by the 1870s, but 'unchanged levels of infant and maternal mortality suggest that antisepsis and obstetrics were unproductive or nullified by interventionist methods in childbirth.' In most cases, midwives were not trained nurses, even if they had undertaken specialist training. The London Obstetrical Society was one of the main trainers of midwives in the London area and it did not insist that applicants were trained nurses.

Calls for the profession to be regulated in a similar way to medical professionals under the 1858 Medical Act were vehemently opposed by male doctors. They feared that qualified midwives represented a significant threat to their livelihoods. In the 1860s, the Female Medical Society had attempted to establish a Licentiate in Midwifery with medical registration, but failed. From the 1880s, the Midwives Institute campaigned for the same goal, and Bills were introduced to Parliament in 1890 and 1899, but failed both times.

Finally, in July 1902, the Midwives Bill was passed and the Central Midwives Board was set up to police it and to maintain a *Midwives Roll* for England and Wales. The new legislation stipulated that no woman could attend a birth for payment from April 1910 unless she was qualified. This eight-year period was designed to allow time for a sufficient number of midwives to be trained. The Central Midwives Board's role was to maintain standards and it had the power to strike off any midwives from the roll who were found guilty of misconduct or misrepresentation.

To become qualified, a midwife had to undertake a training course, which included lectures, written and oral examinations, and attendance at a specified number of births, under supervision. If she passed the course, she received a certificate from a recognised professional body, which was proof of her qualification, and her name was placed on the *Midwives Roll*. According to Stephen Halliday in his article 'Delivering the Goods' in *BBC Who Do You Think You Are?* (December 2007), by 1905 almost 10,000 midwives had qualified.

Although the training was compulsory, it was unpaid, so it was difficult for many women to become qualified as midwives. Once qualified, certified midwives could advertise their services in local directories and publications.

District nurses

The roots of district nursing in Britain lie with William Rathbone, a merchant and philanthropist from Liverpool. In 1859, he employed Mary Robinson to nurse his wife during her terminal illness. After his wife died, he retained Mary Robinson's services for the poor of the city who could not afford to pay for nursing; she visited them in their own homes.

District nurses preparing for their rounds in Edinburgh, 1895. (Courtesy of the Queen's Nursing Institute, Scotland)

After the positive effects of nursing in the home became apparent, William Rathbone worked with Florence Nightingale to develop the service. However, insufficient numbers of trained nurses were available, so Rathbone set up and funded a nursing school in Liverpool specifically to train nurses for the eighteen districts of the city. Other cities like Manchester and Salford took on this idea of 'district nursing' and the Metropolitan and National Nursing Association was set up in 1874.

In rural areas, another organisation, which was the brainchild of Elizabeth Malleson, was also providing relief for the impoverished sick. This was the national charity, the Rural Nursing Association (RNA), which was set up in 1890. Six years earlier, Elizabeth had been forced to close a similar charity, the short-lived Village Nursing Association, due to lack of funds. According to Carrie Howse in *Rural District Nursing in Gloucestershire 1880–1924*, by 1892 the RNA had nurses in seventy-seven districts in twenty-five counties.

The district nursing scheme developed further when, in 1887, women across England were invited to make donations of money and suggest how

JENNY WOLFE, QUEEN'S NURSE

Jenny Wolfe, district nurse, with her donkey and trap at Gotherington, Gloucestershire, 1895. (Courtesy of the Queen's Nursing Institute, London)

Born in Lausanne, Switzerland, in 1855, Jenny Golay married George Wolfe, a shoemaker from Lyndhurst, in 1880. At some point before 1890, she must have decided to become a nurse, but it is not clear if she was still living with her husband at the time.

The *Roll of Queen's Nurses* records that Jenny trained as a nurse in Shrewsbury and completed her district training in Manchester. She was appointed as a Queen's Nurse on 1 January 1894, and, as three years' training had to be completed before applying for district nursing, Jenny must have been training in Shrewsbury from 1890 or 1891. She has not been found on the census for this time, although her husband was recorded as visiting friends on the Isle of Wight.

Jenny Wolfe became the much-loved district nurse for the rural village of Gotherington in Gloucestershire. She served a wide area – in seven months in 1897, she travelled 1,294 miles in her donkey-cart, averaging 185 miles per month. Sadly in 1898, Jenny contracted an illness as a result of her work and died two months later, aged just 43. In *Rural District Nursing in Gloucestershire 1880–1925*, Carrie Howse quotes Elizabeth Malleson as saying that Nurse Wolfe was 'mourned by all who knew her moral rectitude and her unselfish devotion to those who needed her skill and sympathy'. The general remarks in the *Roll of Queen's Nurses* record that her death was 'much regretted by the Committee and patients'.

it could be best spent to mark Queen Victoria's Golden Jubilee. A proposal by William Rathbone and Florence Nightingale was chosen, which set out a plan to nurse the sick poor. The Queen Victoria's Jubilee Institute (QVJI) was founded in 1889, and district nurses were known as 'Queen's Nurses'. The organisation changed its name to the Queen's Institute of District Nursing in 1928, and to the Queen's Nursing Institute in 1973. The success of the Rural Nursing Association made it inevitable that it and the QVJI would pool resources and amalgamate, which they did in 1897, in time for Queen Victoria's Diamond Jubilee.

District nursing was run at a local level by the district nursing associations (DNAs). It was their job to raise sufficient funds to pay the nurses' salaries. The cost was met by two forms of income: subscriptions and charity events such as fetes and jumble sales. Members of each rural community paid yearly subscriptions to take advantage of the service offered by the district nurse, although the old and very poor were nursed free of charge.

At first, it was suggested that between £25 and £30 a year be paid to each district nurse, plus a uniform, laundry and accommodation. It was intended that the living quarters provided should be a cottage for each nurse, though if this was not possible, board and lodgings in two furnished rooms would suffice. By 1909, the minimum wage had increased to £30, with an extra £2 a year if the district nurse practised midwifery. Transport also had to be provided for the district nurse, whether it was a donkey, pony and cart, or bicycle.

As their duties included general nursing, public health work and often midwifery, district nurses required a high level of training. They were trained nurses who had undertaken additional training for district work, and some also had midwifery training. Without recourse to immediate help from a doctor, district nurses had to think on their feet, inspire confidence in their patients and be able to work on their own initiative. When the National Health Service was founded in 1948, home nursing became available to all and district nurses were employed by local authorities.

Health visitors

The role of health visitors was to visit women in their homes and give advice on antenatal care, birth control, hygiene and sanitation, as well as the rearing and management of infants. The emphasis was on education and dispelling myths and 'old wives' tales' that had permeated down through the generations.

In 1907, the Notification of Births Act was passed, which required the inspection of all newborn babies by a health visitor. This became compulsory in 1915 with the Notification of Births (Extension) Act, forcing all councils to employ health visitors in order to comply with the law.

Prior to 1915, some areas had already introduced health visitors. In 1906, Huddersfield set up the first comprehensive health visiting scheme and two years later the London County Council (General Powers) Act empowered sanitary authorities to employ female health visitors. In 1909, the Health Visitors' (London) Order was passed, requiring health visitors to have either a medical degree or the Central Midwives Board certificate, or general nursing training and a health visitor's certificate (a specific qualification for health visitors).

There is an advertisement for a female health visitor on the Walsall History Projects website (www2.walsall.gov.uk/History_Projects). Dated 1916, it specifies that applicants had to be under the age of 40, and needed training and practical experience in caring for infants, as well as a certificate in midwifery. The advertisement stated that preference would be given to candidates 'who also have a certificate as Health Visitor or Sanitary Inspector of the Royal Sanitary Institute, or of the Sanitary Inspector's Examination Board'. The salary, to include the cost of a uniform, was £75 per annum with a war bonus of 3s. a week 'to be increased by £5 a year for meritorious service to £90 a year'.

When the National Health Service was founded in 1948, the role of health visitors extended further, and they became involved with the health of the whole family, not just the mother and infant children.

Mental nurses

Male members of staff in lunatic asylums were known as 'keepers' or attendants, while the females were termed nurses. Before 1890, there were no entry examinations for mental nurses or asylum attendants, but attendants were usually drawn from the working classes, with sufficient physical

A district nurse tending an injured girl in the hop gardens of Herefordshire, 1940s. (Courtesy of the Queen's Nursing Institute, London)

strength to restrain patients if required, and the kinds of skills that would enable them to supervise patients doing work therapy.

According to Robert Dingwall, Anne Marie Rafferty and Charles Webster in *An Introduction to the Social History of Nursing*, 'wages and conditions were modelled on those of domestic or farm servants.' Attendants and nurses were required to be resident in the asylum, and they worked long hours for comparatively little pay. Fourteen-hour days were still common in 1900 and the average salary for an attendant was £30 per annum.

Asylum attendants were responsible for the safety, cleanliness and general condition of the patients, and for the ventilation, warmth and good order of their respective wards. They were encouraged to treat the patients kindly, and never to strike or speak harshly to them.

The rules at Lancaster County Asylum stated there should be no less than one attendant for every twenty-five patients who are tranquil or convalescent, and no less than one attendant for every fifteen patients who are 'dirty, violent, or refractory, or dangerous to themselves or others'. These ratios were the standard that most asylums worked between.

Attendants and mental nurses were also required in Poor Law institutions, where harmless lunatics and imbeciles were often housed: it was cheaper than accommodating them in asylums. From the 1860s, Poor Law unions had to recruit extra staff to look after the ever-increasing numbers housed in workhouses. Many unions employed insufficient paid attendants, relying instead on help provided by some of the sane pauper inmates. Lunacy commissioners visited every institution housing lunatics and imbeciles annually, including workhouses. Although they could pressurise the unions to appoint sufficient staff, it could take years for their recommendations to be implemented.

In order to increase the calibre of candidates for attendant posts, efforts were made to put into place a system of training. In 1885, a text entitled *Handbook for the Instruction of Attendants on the Insane* was produced by a group of Scottish asylum superintendents. This was well regarded by those in charge of asylums and it was adopted by the Medico-Psychological Association (MPA) in 1893. The association added extra material to the text about anatomy, physiology and nursing – three years later, the publication became required reading for the MPA certificate course. By then, it included self-assessment questions and details about training and examinations. In 1923, the title was changed to *Handbook for Mental Nurses*, and it remained the standard work until 1954.

The Certificate of Proficiency in Mental Nursing was introduced in 1890, and, by 1924, 17,429 applicants had passed the examination and received a certificate. However, this represented a very small proportion of asylum staff: just 26 per cent of male staff and 16 per cent of females.

When the 1919 Nurses Registration Act was passed, it included legislation to create a supplementary register of mental nurses. In 1920, the MPA certificate was accepted by the General Nursing Council as a means to be admitted to the new supplementary register. When the NHS was founded in 1948, nearly 80 per cent of male mental nurses were qualified.

Section 3

PATIENTS

Chapter 10

MEDICAL TREATMENT
FOR PATIENTS

Imagine the child of one of your nineteenth-century ancestors was sick, perhaps with a recurrent chest problem. What kind of medical treatment was available to them, and where would they have accessed it? This would really depend on how well off the family were, and what sort of income they had.

The wealthy could request a visit from the very best medical practitioners or, later in the nineteenth century, visit them in their consulting rooms. These practitioners would be the most eminent in their field – usually hospital consultants with a large, successful private practice. Again, the family with a large income could act on any advice given to them – such as having private massage, undertaking hydrotherapy treatment or spending the summer at a spa in the Alps. They could also afford to pay for a private nurse if needed.

If your ancestors were from the middle classes, they too would have been able to afford private medical treatment, but not from a top consultant. They would have taken their child to a general practitioner. The new specialist hospitals, which charged for their services, were also a possible source of treatment if the general practitioner could not solve the problem. Later in the nineteenth century, the large, charitable voluntary hospitals introduced a small number of private beds for paying patients, and a middle-class family could have afforded this if such treatment was necessary. Private nursing may also have been within their budget. The lower middle classes would also have tried their local dispensing chemist for advice.

Skilled craftsmen in regular, well-paid employment could have accessed medical treatment through a sick club or friendly society. If your ancestor was a member, he would have paid a weekly sum into the insurance scheme and, if he became ill, he could receive benefits of around 3s. 6d. to 6s. per week during his time off work. Every sick club had a doctor, who was usually a general practitioner undertaking the work to generate extra income. If he paid an extra fee of around 2s. 6d. each year, your ancestor was also entitled to be attended by the club doctor. However, it was rare for benefits to extend to family members, so being a member would not have helped the sick child in the family.

Your working-class ancestors would not have been able to afford the fees of a qualified general practitioner, even though they were often reduced for the poor. They would have consulted the family 'receipt' book (an archaic term for recipes) handed down by previous generations. The local dispensing chemist or druggist would have made up their receipts for them, or he might have offered suggestions from his own receipt book. From the mid-nineteenth century, commercially prepared patent medicines started to replace herbal remedies. These could be bought from chemists, grocers and general stores.

The family may also have tried to get medical help from an unqualified practitioner such as a herbalist or leechman. Even after the Medical Act of 1858 was passed, these practitioners, labelled as 'quacks' by the medical profession, were still legally able to peddle their wares, in person or by post.

If your ancestors were just above the poverty line, they could have sought free treatment for their child at the charitable voluntary hospital, which was staffed by the same consultant physicians and surgeons who treated the rich. These consultants worked on an unpaid, part-time basis at the voluntary hospitals to increase the prestige of their private practices, and to teach the medical students.

However, in order for their child to be seen at a voluntary hospital, your ancestors would have had to get a recommendation for hospital treatment from a subscriber, stating they were a 'fit object' for charity. Subscribers were wealthy members of the community who paid an annual subscription, which entitled them to recommend a set number of in- or out-patients to the hospital every year. Making charitable contributions to hospitals in this way emphasised the high social status of subscribers, and their names were recorded in the annual reports produced by individual hospitals for everyone to see. Recommendations were also known as letters, tickets or, in Scotland, a 'line'. The recommendation rule did not apply for emergency cases such as accidents.

The identity of subscribers in the community would have been common knowledge, so the family could have applied to one of them personally for a recommendation, or perhaps through a clergyman or general practitioner. The same system of recommendation by subscribers was used by specialist hospitals and those specifically for women and children.

If the hospital deemed that the family could afford to pay for medical treatment, their child would have been refused admission. If this happened, the family could have tried their local dispensary, which was also staffed by qualified medical practitioners. They were mainly an urban phenomenon and many towns had separate dispensaries, while most Scottish hospitals had a dispensary attached – similar to an out-patient department that operated a system of home visiting.

Voluntary general hospitals, funded by charity, were founded to serve the industrious poor, not paupers. If your English or Welsh ancestors were receiving poor relief, they would have been barred from the voluntary hospitals and were expected to take their child to the Poor Law infirmary. In some cases, perhaps if specialist treatment could not be provided at the workhouse, paupers could be recommended for treatment at a voluntary hospital by the guardians of the Poor Law union.

The operating theatre at the 2nd Northern General Hospital, Leeds, May 1915. (Author's collection)

In Scotland, there was a different poor relief system. The family could have applied for medical treatment through the poorhouse, and medical relief would have been given to the sick child at home. If hospital treatment was required, the child would have been sent to the local voluntary hospital, recommended by the poorhouse authorities. By the end of the nineteenth century, it was more common for the sick poor to be admitted to the poorhouse on medical grounds, instead of receiving treatment at home.

Going into hospital

Let's imagine that your ancestor's sick child has a recommendation for treatment at the voluntary hospital. What was it like inside? The family would first have gone to the out-patients department, where the junior medical staff separated the serious and interesting cases from the more mundane. While most people visiting the department were attending for one-off treatment, many were patients with ongoing out-patient appointments. Treatment as an out-patient was not always medical, as the hospitals supplied surgical appliances such as crutches, artificial limbs, spectacles or trusses.

The out-patients department operated in a similar way to today's accident and emergency department. Cases were examined, and if they could not be treated there and then, or if further investigation was required, patients were admitted to the hospital.

Some prospective in-patients would have already been recommended for treatment inside the hospital and they would have an admission ticket, which stated the day and time they had to arrive. The ticket also listed the personal items in-patients were expected to bring with them, which varied from place to place, but might include a change of clothing, plus nightclothes, a knife, fork and spoon, or a comb and brush.

In hospital, patients were admitted to either a medical or surgical ward and assigned to a particular consultant. Your ancestor's sick child with the chest problem would have been admitted to a medical ward at first. The admission ticket entitled the child to treatment for a maximum of six weeks under one ticket. A liberal diet and plenty of bedrest was all that many impoverished patients needed to recover from illness. After six weeks, the surgeon or physician in charge of the case could renew the ticket if he deemed it necessary. Later in the nineteenth century, patients were often discharged to hospital-owned convalescent homes for further recuperation.

Your ancestors would probably have worried less about their child being in hospital as a medical case than if surgery was required. Between the 1840s and the 1870s, post-operative death rates from 'hospital diseases' – such as hospital gangrene, erysipelas (also known as St Anthony's Fire) and pyaemia, as well as shock – were extremely high. A 35 per cent death rate was common. As the nineteenth century progressed, a better understanding of how these diseases were transmitted, as well as the introduction of aseptic and antiseptic techniques, cut these death rates dramatically. From 1850, anaesthetics such as ether, chloroform or laughing gas were routinely used, so that pain-free operations became the norm.

Every hospital was governed by a strict set of rules, which applied to staff, patients and visitors. Anyone who disobeyed the rules was considered refractory and 'disorderly' and could be punished by being discharged for 'irregularities'. Most hospitals had similar rules that banned smoking or chewing tobacco, cursing or swearing, gambling or drinking spirituous liquors.

Convalescents at the London. (*The Sphere,* 13 June 1903)

Other healthcare providers

In the eighteenth and early nineteenth centuries, hospitals provided medical treatment, food, shelter and time for convalescence. As yet, there were no medical procedures that could not be carried out at home. Most general hospitals refused to admit those with infectious diseases because they could not be cured, and admitting them would only lead to further outbreaks of disease. In Scotland, however, the voluntary general hospitals accepted all cases needing medical treatment, with separate wards for fever and smallpox patients.

By the last quarter of the nineteenth century, there was a wide range of places offering medical treatment, in addition to general and specialist hospitals, and dispensaries. By the 1880s, cottage hospitals were increasingly common in rural areas, while isolation hospitals for patients with infectious diseases were set up in the 1860s and 1870s. Private convalescent homes were available for those who could afford to pay for the treatment, as were hydropathic spa resorts. For those afflicted with mental illness, public lunatic asylums accommodated pauper patients, while private institutions offered more comfort to those with substantial incomes.

Towards the NHS

Although workers on low pay were entitled to free healthcare under the National Insurance Act of 1911, their wives and children were not, so they still had to pay for medical treatment or go to a voluntary hospital. Better-paid workers and the retired were also not covered. The out-patients departments of voluntary hospitals were extremely popular – according to Geoffrey Rivett on his National Health Service History website (www.nhshistory.net), 6 million people a year were attending them by 1939.

By the 1920s, local authorities were in charge of midwifery services, mental hospitals, sanatoria for tuberculosis patients, and hospitals for infectious diseases such as diphtheria and scarlet fever. Under the Local Government Act of 1929, local authorities had the power to take over Poor Law institutions and develop them into better hospitals.

From 1944, the school health service was responsible for all dental and medical treatment for children in maintained schools. By 1948, under the NHS, everyone was entitled to free healthcare including dental treatment and eye tests.

Section 4

SOURCES

Chapter 11
GENERAL SOURCES

The census

The census is an official count of the population, and the first one in Britain was taken on 10 March 1801; a census has been taken every ten years since, except 1941. Public access to census return data is usually restricted for 100 years, and the dates on which the currently available census returns were taken are: 6 June 1841; 30 March 1851; 7 April 1861; 2 April 1871; 3 April 1881; 5 April 1891; 31 March 1901; and 2 April 1911. The 1911 census is not yet fully available across the UK, although it will be by 2012. For England and Wales, much of it can be accessed online for a fee.

The first useful census for family historians is the one taken in 1841, as the previous returns were mainly for statistical purposes. However, this census does not provide as much information as those in later years because the ages of adults over 15 were rounded down to the nearest five years, and places of birth were not given – simply an 'N' for no and 'Y' for yes to the question 'Were you born in this county?'

Later census returns give the full address, the full name of the householder and everyone in the household (plus their relationship to the head of the house); their ages, condition as to marriage, place of birth and occupation; if blind, deaf or dumb, and later, if an idiot or lunatic. From 1891, information is given about the number of rooms occupied if less than five, and whether individuals were an employer, employed or neither. This was slightly changed in 1901 to read 'Employer, Worker or Own Account' or 'Working at Home'.

Each place was divided into a number of enumeration districts covered by individual enumerators, so unless you use an online search facility, you will need to know roughly where your ancestor was living.

Census returns for England and Wales are freely available at the National Archives, and, for specific areas, at county record offices and large city libraries. Scottish census returns can be accessed at the ScotlandsPeople Centre (www.scotlandspeoplehub.gov.uk/index) or at county record offices.

You can also see census returns on many commercial family history websites on a subscription or pay-per-view basis. Many archives and libraries subscribe to these websites, so it is often possible to use the service for free. The beauty of this format is that it makes the census easily searchable by place or name, but be aware it is always possible that your ancestor's name was incorrectly transcribed, leading to a 'not found' scenario.

Don't underestimate the value of the census in researching your medical ancestors. For doctors, it can show if he or she was working in private practice, or in a hospital or other institution, and as a surgeon or a physician. Medical professionals often gave the census enumerator their precise medical qualifications, job titles and where they qualified.

If your doctor ancestor was a house surgeon or physician at a hospital, he or she would have lived on the premises. If you can't find your ancestor on a particular census, it's worth trying large city hospitals, asylums or

Sir Andrew Clark's house. (The Strand Magazine, 1893)

workhouses/poorhouses in case he or she was on the staff; these institutions usually had their own registration district.

For medical professionals with families, look carefully at the birthplaces of their children. Moving to another part of the country to secure a better post was a common occurrence for an ambitious doctor. Children's birthplaces give an indication of the different areas where your ancestor worked, and a starting point for research in the surviving staff records of hospitals. Children may even have been born abroad, possibly indicating that your ancestor spent time in the army or navy medical services.

The neighbourhood itself where your doctor was living at the time of the census can reveal much about his or her career. Established doctors in private practice tended to live close to one another in a kind of 'medical quarter'. Look at the neighbours in the same street. Do they follow the same profession, or are they of a similar professional standing? If not, your doctor was probably not yet well established enough to afford to live in such an area. The type and number of servants living in the household can also give an indication of wealth – for instance, if there is a stable boy or groom, your ancestor may have had his own carriage.

For nurses, the census can tell you where your ancestor trained or worked, or whether she was a specific type of nurse. Again, nurses moved around the country for better posts or to undertake training, so don't be surprised if your ancestor is not where you expect her to be.

Trade directories

Like today's telephone directories, old trade directories were made up of people offering goods and services in a particular area, who paid to be listed. They were usually published for each county or large city, although late eighteenth- and early nineteenth-century directories often covered several counties in one volume.

Trade directories can be useful in helping to corroborate information found in censuses or other sources. They can also help to fill in the gaps if your doctor ancestor was practising between 1784 and 1845, when no medical registers were produced. Early directories listed surgeons and other medical professions alphabetically with other trades, while later versions had a specific 'Medical List' that appeared before the main trades. You will need to check the contents page of each directory to see how it is arranged, as they can be subtly different.

It's possible to find nurses listed in trade directories, especially if they were working in private nursing. From the end of the nineteenth century onwards, school nurses started to be listed under the sections dedicated to educational committees for specific areas.

A useful online source of old trade directories is the Historical Directories project (www.historicaldirectories.org). A selection from a number of different counties and decades have been digitised, and you may find that the area you're interested in has been covered. When searching using the key word 'nurse', bear in mind that 'Nurse' can also be a surname.

Most county record offices, archives or large city libraries have a selection of old trade directories. Some of the larger libraries even have collections that cover the whole country.

Obituaries

Finding an obituary for your ancestor can really help to fill in the gaps and paint a picture of what he or she was like as a person. Lengthy obituaries can be like gold-dust, including information about place of birth and death, places of work and where the deceased trained or studied, as well as personal anecdotes and tributes from friends and colleagues. There may even be a funeral report listing mourners and their relationship to the deceased. Shorter obituaries simply state the date of birth and death.

For doctors, you may find journals – such as the *Lancet* (from 1823) or the *British Medical Journal* (from 1828) – will have an obituary for your ancestor. There is also the *Medical Times*, which later became the *Medical Times and Gazette* and was published between 1839 and 1885. The *Glasgow Medical Journal* (from 1828) and the *Edinburgh Medical Journal* (from 1805) are worth checking if your medical ancestor was Scottish.

Archived issues of the *British Medical Journal* can be viewed online at (www.bmj.com/search) or PubMed (http://ukpmc.ac.uk). The database can be searched by date and name; large reference libraries may also have copies. Back copies of the *Lancet* can be viewed at the Wellcome Library.

The Times and the *Gentleman's Magazine* also published obituaries. You can view *The Times* archive online using your library card if your local library is a subscriber to it; you do not have to be in the library to view it. There is an index to the obituaries that appeared in the *Gentleman's Magazine* between 1781 and 1819 in the Wellcome Library.

For nurses, you may find an obituary in the *Nursing Record*, which started in 1888. It became the *British Journal of Nursing* from 1902, running until 1956. The RCN Archives has digitised the whole run of the journal (www.rcn.org.uk/development/rcn_archives/historical_nursing_journals) so you can easily search it by name for your ancestor.

The local newspaper for the area in which your ancestor lived may also have marked his or her death. For cities, try 18th and 19th Century Newspapers Online (http://newspapers.bl.uk/blcs), which has digitised forty-nine local and national titles – you may be lucky enough to find the place you're interested in has been covered. This is a subscription website but many libraries subscribe to it, so it may be possible to view it for free with your library card.

Alternatively, the local record office should hold copies of relevant newspapers and may even have name indexes to help narrow down the search. You can find out where your nearest archive is through ARCHON (www.nationalarchives.gov.uk/archon).

Wills for England and Wales

If your ancestor left a will, it can be extremely useful in helping to determine family relationships. Before 12 January 1858, there was no national court for proving English and Welsh wills. Instead, they were proved in one of more than 250 church courts. Most of these documents are held in county record offices; you can search Access to Archives (A2A) to find out about specific probate records held at individual archives (www.a2a.org.uk).

The National Archives holds the original indexes to wills and administrations of the Prerogative Court of Canterbury, catalogued under PROB 12. You can also search them on Documents Online (www.nationalarchives.gov.uk/documentsonline/wills.asp); a fee is payable to download each document.

Online will indexes for other church courts/record offices are listed on Your Archives (http://yourarchives.nationalarchives.gov.uk/index.php?title=Online_Probate_Indexes).

Wills proved in England and Wales from 12 January 1858 are held by the Probate Service. The National Probate Calendar is an index of these wills and administrations; the full index can be seen at the London Probate Registry, while partial indexes are available at the National Archives, the Guildhall Library, the Society of Genealogists and local probate registries. A list of these can be found on the Probate Registry website (www.hmcourts-service.gov.uk/infoabout/civil/probate/registries).

The entries in the National Probate Calendar give the full name, address and occupation of the deceased; the full names of executors, administrators and relationships to the deceased; the date and place of death, and of the granting of probate or administration; plus the value of the estate. An application for administration could be made if a person died without leaving a will and there were problems with the estate. If your ancestor left a will, it should have been proved within a year or two of his or her death.

Once you have the exact details of your ancestor's will or administration, you can apply for a copy in person at the London Probate Registry, or by post from the York Probate Sub-Registry (see the Useful Contacts section).

Wills for Scotland

In Scotland, the terminology for wills is slightly different. The term 'testament' is used to describe documents that relate to the executry of the deceased, including an inventory and, in a minority of cases, a will.

Testaments for the period 1514–1901 have been digitised, and can be seen at the National Archives of Scotland. Alternatively, you can search the free online index on the ScotlandsPeople website (www.scotlandspeople.gov.uk); a charge is made for buying copies of documents.

From 1902, there is an annual index of Scottish testaments called the Calendar of Confirmations. The Calendar is available at The National Archives for Scotland, and the Mitchell Library in Glasgow, which holds the index up to 1936.

Biographical sources

If your ancestor was a well-known figure, check *Who Was Who* and *The Oxford Dictionary of National Biography* in case there is a reference to him or her. Both should be available in large city libraries, and an online version of the latter can be viewed using your library card if your library subscribes to it.

Chapter 12

SOURCES FOR PHYSICIANS, SURGEONS AND APOTHECARIES

Before the Medical Act was passed in 1858, the term 'medical practitioner' was very loosely applied to physicians, surgeons and apothecaries. From the second quarter of the nineteenth century, a new breed of practitioner called surgeon-apothecaries became common. They were akin to today's general practitioners and had qualifications as a surgeon and an apothecary. A medical practitioner could therefore fall into two or more categories, so it is advisable to check at least printed sources for physicians, surgeons and apothecaries.

Before starting your research, download the 'Biographical and Family History Resources in the Wellcome Library' guide on the Wellcome Library website (http://library.wellcome.ac.uk/assets/wtx049847.pdf). It provides an excellent overview of the sources available to trace all kinds of medical professionals.

The *Medical Directory* (from 1846) and the *Medical Register* (from 1859)

The *Medical Register* and *Medical Directory* should be your first port of call when starting your research. These annual publications list medical practitioners qualified to practise their profession in Britain and the colonies, even if they were working abroad. This means you can trace your ancestor's career, year on year.

Both publications can usually be consulted at large city libraries or specialist medical archives; selected records can also be seen online on a subscription or pay-per-view basis. Ancestry (www.ancestry.co.uk) has digitised the *Medical Register* from 1859–1959 at four-year intervals, i.e. 1859, 1863, 1867 and so on. Family Relatives (www.familyrelatives.com) has a selection of both the *Medical Register* and the *Medical Directory*.

The two publications are different. The *Medical Directory* was produced by a commercial printer and it was not compulsory to be listed in it, while the

Hig—Hil]   THE MEDICAL REGISTER for 1896.   663

Name.	Address.	Date and Place of Registration.	Qualifications.
HIGGINSON, Frederick William.	2, Eden park, Sandycove, Co. Dublin.	1861, Nov. 9 E.	Lic., Lic. Midwif. 1861, Fell. 1882, R. Coll. Surg. Irel. Lic. Med. Univ. Dubl., 1865.
HIGGINSON, George	Ragleth house, Church Stretton, Salop.	1894, Jan. 4 E.	Lic. Soc. Apoth. Lond., 1893. Mem. R. Coll. Surg. Eng., 1895. Lic. R. Coll. Phys. Lond., 1895.
HIGGINSON, John Wigmore	Thornleigh, Stoneygate, Leicester.	1890, Jan. 22 E.	Mem. R. Coll. Surg. Eng., 1889. Lic. R. Coll. Phys. Lond., 1889.
HIGGS, Augustus William	18, Wellington square, Chelsea, London. S.W.	1874, Sept. 15 E.	Lic. Soc. Apoth. Lond., 1874. Lic. R. Coll. Surg. Edin., 1876.
HIGGS, Alfred	57, London road, Leicester.	1878, April 23 E.	Mem. R. Coll. Surg. Eng., 1878. Lic. Soc. Apoth. Lond., 1878.
HIGGS, Ernest William Mules.	Friary house, Bodmin, Cornwall.	1891, Nov. 13 E.	Mem. R. Coll. Surg. Eng., 1891. Lic. R. Coll. Phys. Lond., 1891.
HIGGS, Thomas Frederic ...	Beaconsfield house, Dudley.	1859, Jan. 1 E.	Mem. R. Coll. Surg. Eng., 1858. Lic. R. Coll. Phys. Edin., 1860. Lic. Soc. Apoth. Lond., 1860. M.D. Univ. St. And., 1884.
HIGGS, Walter Alpheus ...	Guy's Hospital, London. S.E.	1892, Feb. 26 E.	Mem. R. Coll. Surg. Eng., 1892. Lic. R. Coll. Phys. Lond., 1892.
HIGHET, Campbell	Hollybank, Dalmellington, Ayrshire.	1893, Jan. 21 S.	M.B., Mast. Surg. 1892, Univ. Glasg.
HIGHET, Hugh	1, Gordon terrace, Cork.	1895, May 15 S.	Lic. R. Coll. Phys. Edin., 1895. Lic. R. Coll. Surg. Edin., 1895. Lic. Fac. Phys. Surg. Glasg., 1895.
HIGHET, Hugh Campbell...	The Dispensary, Singapore.	1888, Oct. 26 S.	M.B., Mast. Surg. 1888, M.D. 1892, Univ. Glasg.
HIGHET, John	Langlands house, South Beach, Troon, Ayrshire.	1872, July 25 S.	Lic. Fac. Phys. Surg. Glasg., 1872. M.B. 1876, M.D. Mast. Surg. 1884, Univ. Glasg. Dip. Publ. Health R. Colls. Phys. Surg. Edin., & Fac. Phys. Surg. Glasg., 1893.
HIGHET, John	Allonby house, Workington, Cumberland.	1875, Mar. 15 S.	M.B., Mast. Surg. 1873, M.D. 1883, Univ. Glasg.
HIGHET, Robert Campbell	9, Havelock terrace, Ayr	1886, Aug. 20 S.	M.B., Mast. Surg. 1886, Univ. Glasg.
HIGHETT, Charles............	Field house, Richmond road, Montpelier, Bristol.	1859, Jan. 1 E.	Lic. Soc. Apoth. Lond., 1840. Lic. 1860, Mem. 1865, R. Coll. Phys. Edin.
HIGNETT, Lionel Watson...	Donebmir, Campsie, Londonderry.	1892, Oct. 27 E.	Mem. R. Coll. Surg. Eng., 1892. Lic. R. Coll. Phys. Lond., 1892.
HIGHMOOR, Richard Nicolson.	Guiseley, near Leeds	1886, Aug. 2 E.	M.B., Mast. Surg. 1886, Univ. Edin.
HIGHTON, Thomas............	Green hill house, Normanton road, Derby.	1874, Feb. 6 E.	Mem. R. Coll. Surg. Eng., 1873. Lic. Soc. Apoth. Lond., 1875.
HIGSON, James	87, Preston New road, Blackburn.	1879, Sept. 20 E.	Mem. R. Coll. Surg. Eng., 1879. Lic. Soc. Apoth. Lond., 1879.
HIGSON, John Russell......	Oakmere, Honor oak park, London. S.E.	1893, Feb. 20 S.	M.B., Mast. Surg. 1892, Univ. Edin.
HILBARD, George Franklin	131, Lichfield street, Walsall.	1888, April 23 S.	Lic. R. Coll. Phys. Edin., 1888. Lic. R. Coll. Surg. Edin., 1888. Lic. Fac. Phys. Surg. Glasg., 1888.
HILBERS, Hermann Gerhard	49, Montpelier road, Brighton.	1885, Nov. 4 E.	Lic. R. Coll. Phys. Edin., 1885. Lic. R. Coll. Surg. Edin., 1885. Lic. Fac. Phys. Surg. Glasg., 1885.

Entry for Thomas Frederic Higgs in the 1896 Medical Register. (Courtesy of Familyrelatives.com)

Medical Register was published by the General Medical Council after the 1858 Medical Act was passed, and it was obligatory for all practising medical professionals to be registered in it, hence the name. The content is also quite different, with much more information provided in the *Medical Directory*. Ideally, both sources should be checked for the period of time in which your ancestor was practising to compare and corroborate details.

Both publications provide full names, address, and the exact date of qualifications. The *Medical Register* also states when each individual registered, if this was later. This helps to differentiate between people with the same or common name, when you are not sure which address is correct.

If the address given was at a hospital, your ancestor probably had a house position, living and working on site. If it's a private address, he or she was in private practice, usually with consulting rooms in their own home. Over the course of a career, addresses inevitably changed, so read each entry carefully. For some entries, two addresses are given, but this was usually after a medical professional had fully established himself in private practice, and could afford a separate address for his consulting rooms.

Some entries record when a medical professional is actually retired, but in most cases, the entries continue until his or her death. It is therefore not always clear when an individual stopped practising medicine.

At first, the *Medical Directory* was printed as the *London and Provincial Medical Directory*, with separate volumes for Scotland and Ireland. However, all the countries were amalgamated into one volume from the 1850s under the title *London and Provincial Medical Directory, inclusive of Ireland and Scotland*.

Unlike the *Medical Register*, the *Medical Directory* is split into sections: the London Medical Directory; the Provincial Medical Directory; the Medical Directory for Scotland; the Medical Directory for Ireland; Army and Navy, Indian Medical Service and Mercantile Marine; Practitioners Resident Abroad Possessing British Qualifications; and Licentiates in Dental Surgery. Each section is arranged alphabetically by surname.

If you can't find your ancestor in the London or Provincial sections, check all the others in case he spent time as a military medical officer or practised abroad. There is also a 'Too Late List' at the front which should be checked as well; this lists those who returned their details too late to be included in the main sections.

At the back of each volume, there is an obituary section and a memorial section with longer obituaries, as well as lists of staff of the major hospitals, especially those in London.

The *Medical Register* is arranged alphabetically by surname without any additional sections. Medical practitioners who were practising abroad can be found mixed together with those working in Britain. For every individual, the *Medical Register* provides their full name, address, the date of registration with the General Medical Council (and later the place: e.g. E for England, S for Scotland, I for Ireland), plus the precise medical qualifications they had attained.

These qualifications are recorded in an abbreviated format which, at first glance, can appear to be a new kind of language. There are tables of abbreviations listed at the front of each register, and there is a list in Appendix 2 of this book.

For example, the 1896 *Medical Register* lists John Highet of Langlands House, South Beach, Troon, Ayrshire as registering on 25 July 1872 in Scotland. Here are his abbreviated qualifications (the full qualifications are listed in bold):

Lic Fac Phys Surg Glasg 1872
Licentiate of the Faculty of Physicians and Surgeons of Glasgow, 1872

MB 1876, MD Mast Surg 1884, Univ Glasg
Bachelor of Medicine 1876, University of Glasgow
Doctor of Medicine and Master in Surgery 1884, University of Glasgow

Dip Publ Health R Colls Phys Surg Edin & Fac Phys Surg Glasg 1893
Diploma in Public Health, the Royal College of Physicians and Surgeons of Edinburgh and the Faculty of Physicians and Surgeons of Glasgow, 1893

John Highet's first medical qualification in 1872 was that of Licentiate of the Faculty of Physicians and Surgeons of Glasgow. This entitled him to be included in the *Medical Register*. However, he did not attain his first degree – the Bachelor of Medicine – until 1876 from the University of Glasgow. This was followed in 1884 with the Doctor of Medicine and Master in Surgery from the University of Glasgow. John took another qualification in 1893 – the Diploma in Public Health – which would have enabled him to apply for medical officer of health posts.

The long gaps between John's qualifications highlight the fact that it's important to check the *Medical Register* at regular intervals, perhaps every three or four years, to see if new qualifications had been added. The *Register* should be checked more frequently if you wish to record the address of your ancestor for each year; our ancestors moved more often than is usually supposed.

The *Medical Register* does not only list mid-Victorian medical professionals. Anyone practising as a surgeon, physician or apothecary in 1859 and onwards had to be registered with the General Medical Council. This included those who had qualified years before and were still practising, though they paid a reduced fee to register. For instance, the man who had the distinction of appearing first in the 1859 *Medical Register* was Robert Abbotson of Burton, Westmoreland. Although his date of registration is 1 January 1859, his qualification date is given as 1797, as he became a member of the Royal College of Surgeons of England in that year. The obituary section in the back of the 1862 *Medical Directory* notes that Robert died on 7 December 1860 at the age of 87.

Although it was not compulsory to be listed in the *Medical Directory*, it can provide more valuable information than the *Medical Register*. Details include additional posts held – such as vaccinator, Poor Law medical officer and factory surgeon – as well as lists of previous posts and any papers written for medical journals. Previous posts held were labelled as 'late': e.g. late house surgeon at the Cardiff Royal Infirmary.

Where possible, details in the *Medical Register* and the *Medical Directory* should always be cross-checked with other sources such as censuses and trade directories. As with all official records, mistakes and omissions occur and there are instances where known practising doctors are not in the *Medical Register* when they should have been listed, or where address details are incorrect. The onus was on the individual to update the General Medical Council with their correct address details. If your ancestor had a double-barrelled name, check both names individually as well as the double-barrelled version.

Edward Roberts Smith is one surgeon whose details in the *Medical Register* are incorrect. He was born in 1843, the eldest son of Edward Fisher Smith, coal and iron agent for the Earl of Dudley. His medical education began when he was apprenticed to his uncle, Samuel Fereday of Dudley, in whose household he was living at the time of the 1861 census.

Edward registered with the General Medical Council on 15 April 1865 having gained an MRCS (1864) and an LM (Lic Midwif 1865). He became a licentiate of the Society of Apothecaries the following year. The *Medical Register* records him at St Bartholomew's Hospital in London in 1867 and

Higgs   THE MEDICAL DIRECTORY, 1904.

Physiol. Schol.1877; Surg. Schol.1878; Surg.Leic.Provid. Disp., Foresters, &c.

HIGGS, ERNEST WM. MULES, 88, James-st. Oxford (*Teleph.* 0371)—M.R.C.S., L.R.C.P. Lond. 1891 ; L.M. Dub. 1892; (*Char. Cross*); Med. Off. Juv. Foresters; late Demonst. in Minor Surg. and House Surg. Char. Cross Hosp. and Surg. Roy. Niger Co. W. Africa.

HIGGS, THOS. FREDERIC, Beaconsfield House, High-st. Dudley, Worcestersh. (*Teleph.* 62)—M.D. St. And. 1884 ; L.R.C.P. Edin. (exam.) 1860; M.R.C.S. Eng. 1858; L.S.A.1860;(*Syd.Coll.Birm.*);J.P.;Sen.Hon.Surg.Dudley Disp.; Surg. Dudley and Boro' Police; Med. Off. Dudley Union Workh.; Pub.Vacc. Dudley Town Dist.; Med. Off. Post Off.; Exam. to Educat. Departm.; Mem. (Chairm. Dudley Div.Birm.) Br. Brit.Med.Assoc.; late Surg.Dudley Truss Soc. Contrib. "Case of Tertian Ague, with an enlarged and tender Spleen—Recovery," *Lancet.*

HIGGS, WALTER ALPHEUS, Castle Combe, Chippenham, Wilts.—M.R.C.S., L.R.C.P. Lond. 1892 ; (*Guy's*) Med.Off. and Pub.Vacc.Castle Combe Dist. Chippenham Union ; Med. Off. Wilts. Friendly Soc., &c.

HIGHET, JOHN,39,Brow Top, Workington, Cumbld. —M.D. Glasg. 1883, M.B., C.M. 1873 ; (*Univ. Glasg.*); Surg. Workington Disp.; Med. Off. Health Workington U. Dist.; Certif. Fact. Surg. Author of "State Obligations in Matters of Public Health." Contrib. "Cancer of the Pancreas," *Brit. Med. Journ.* 1903.

HIGHMOOR,RICHD.NICOLSON, Litcham, Swaffham, Norfolk—M.B., C.M. Edin.1886 ; (*Edin.* and *Guy's*); Med. Off. and Pub. Vacc. Fransham Dist. and Pub. Vacc. Litcham Dist. Milford and Launditch Union.

HIGHMORE,NATHANIEL JARVIS,Hardibrow,Alumhurst-rd. Bournemouth—M.D. St. And. 1851; M.R.C.S. Eng. 1843 ; L.S.A. 1842 ; (*St. Geo.*)

HIGHTON,Thomas, Green Hill House, Normantonrd.Derby—M.R.C.S. Eng. 1873 ; L.S.A. 1875; (*St. Thos.*); Mem. Brit. Med. Assoc.; late Surg. Derby Disp. ; House Phys. St. Thos. Hosp. 1873-4; Sen. House Surg. Derbysh. Gen. Infirm. 1874-9.

HIGNETT, LIONEL WATSON, Northwood, Middlx. —M.B., C.M. Edin.1896; M.R.C.S., L.R.C.P. Lond.1892; (*Univ. Edin.*); late House Surg. Liverp. Roy. Infirm., and Surg. Pacific S.N. Co. and P. & O. S.N. Co.

HIGSON; THOMAS,87, Preston New-rd. Blackburn—M.R.C.S., L.R.C.P.Lond.1900; (*Owens Coll.*); Mem. Path. Soc. Manch. and Blackburn and Dist. Med. Soc.

HILBERS, HERMANN GERHARD, 49, Montpelier-rd. Brighton—B.A. Camb. 1879 ; L.R.C.P., L.R.C.S. Edin., L.F.P.S. Glasg. 1885 ; (*Guy's*).

HILDIGE, HY. JOHNSTON, Brookfield, Pinner,Middlx. —L.R.C.P.I. and L.M., L.R.C.S.I. and L.M. 1888 ; (*R.C.S.I.*); Mem. W. Herts. Med. Assoc. and Brit. Med. Assoc.;Surg. Hearts of Oak and Odd Fells; late Res. Surg. Pupil and Clin. Clerk Meath Hosp. Contrib. "Case of Internal Obstruction," *Brit. Med. Journ.* 1901.

*HILDYARD, NATHANIEL, 74, Marine Parade, Worthing—L.S.A. 1889.

· *HILDYARD, ROBT. LOXHAM, Halewood, Eastbourne—M.R.C.S. Eng.1886 ; L.S.A.1884 ; (*King's Coll. Lond.* and *Univ. Durh.*)

HILL, ALEX, Downing College Lodge, Cambridge—M.A. Camb., M.D. 1885, M.B. 1882 ; M.R.C.S. Eng. 1880; (*Camb.* and *St. Bart.*); Master of Downing Coll. ; Vice-Chancellor of Camb. Univ. 1897-99 ; J.P. ; Lect. in Adv. Anat. Univ. Camb.; late Demonst. of Anat. and Teacher of Physiol.Univ.Camb.; Hunt. Prof. R.C.S.Eng. and Pres. Neurol.Soc. and Cambs. and Hunts. Br. Brit. Med. Assoc. Author of "The Plan of the Central Nervous System;" "The Physiologist's Note Book;" "A Run Round the Empire;" "Introduction to Science;" "Primer of Physiology." Transl. of Obersteiner's "Central Nervous Organs." Contrib. to *Amer. Syst. of Dis. of Eye*, *Philos. Trans. Roy. Soc.*, *Journ. Anat. and Physiol.*, *Brit. Med. Journ., Brain*, &c.

HILL, ALFRED,Oakwood, Acocks Green, Birmingham —M.D.King's Coll.Aberd.1854; M.R.C.S.Eng. and L.S.A. 1850;(*Birm.*);F.R.S.E.;F.C.S.;F.I.C.; Past Pres.Soc.Med. Offs. Health and Soc. Pub. Analysts; Fell. Sanit. Inst.; Mem. Brit. Med. Assoc.; Pres. Birm. Dist. Counc. Nat. Registr. of Plumbers; formerly Med. Off. Health and AnalystCity of Birm.; Exam. in Pub. Health, Chem. and Med.Jurisp.Univ.Aberd.; Prof.of Chem.and Toxicol.Qu. Coll.,and Lect. on Chem.Birm.and Edgbast.Prop.School. Author of "Reports on the Health of the Borough of Bir-

700

mingham," 1873-1902; "What is the Relation of Water Supply in Large Towns to the Health of the Inhabitants?" "The Chemistry of the Mine;" "House Drains in Relation to Health ;" "The Better Regulation of House Building Generally, and the Best Mode of Improving the Sanitary Condition of Existing Houses ;" "The Notification of Infectious Disease, its Importance and its Difficulties " (Internat. Health Exhib.), 1884 ; "Sewage-Farm Milk and Butter," *Analyst*, 1885 ; " Sewage and House Refuse Disposal in Towns," *Trans. Soc. Med. Offs. Health*, 1887; " The Sanitary Situation," *Ibid.* 1888 ; "Polluted Drinking Water and the Closure of Wells," *Analyst*, 1888; "Diseased Meat," *Trans. Congr. Sanit. Inst.*1894; "Diphtheria," *Ibid.* 1896; " Food Preservatives," *Ibid.* 1898 ; "Tinct. Benzoini Co." *Analyst*,1901 ; "Cremation," *Pub. Health*, 1902.

HILL, ALFRED ARTHUR, Tunstall, Staffs. (*Teleph.* 17 X 2 Central)—L.R.C.P., L.R.C.S. Edin., L.F.P.S. Glasg. 1893; (*Anderson's Coll. Glasg.*); Surg. N. Staffs. Provid. Assoc.;Certif.Fact.Surg.; Med.Ref. Pearl and other Insur. Cos.; Mem.Counc. Brit.Med.Temp. Assoc. Contrib. "Case of Lipoma of Vulva," *Med. Times*, 1894 ; "Medical Temperance Work in the Potteries," *Med. Temp. Rev.* 1901.

HILL, ALFRED BOSTOCK, Ducie House, Olton, Birmingham, and 14, Temple-st. Birmingham (*Teleph.* 04536 Birmingham)—M.Sc. Birm. 1901; M.D. Giessen 1876 ; L.R.C.P. Edin. and L.M. 1876; L.R.C.S. Edin. and L.M. 1884 ; L.S.A. 1876 ; D.P.H. Camb. 1881; (*Qu. Coll. Birm.*); Medals in Chem., Bot. and For. Med.; F.I.C. ; Fell.,Mem. Counc. and Exam. Sanit. Inst.; Ex-Pres.Midl. Br. and Mem. Counc. Soc. Med. Offs. Health ; Mem. Soc. Pub. Analysts, Midl. Med. Soc. and Brit. Med. Assoc.; Emerit. Prof.of Chem. Qu. Coll. Birm.; Prof.of Hyg. and Pub. Health and Lect. on Toxicol. Univ. Birm.; Lect. on Laws of Health Saltley Train. Coll.; Med. Off. Health Warwick Co., Erdington U.D.C., Castle Bromwich R.D.C. and Sutton-Coldfield Boro' ; Analyst for Warwick Co. and Boro', Leamington, Coventry, Hereford City, and Shrewsbury ; Cons. Chemist Warwicksh. and Northamptonsh. Agric. Socs., and Northampton. Chamber of Agric.; formerly Govt. Exam. in Chem. and Physics Bd. Mining Dist. S. Staffs. Author of "Filtration and its Effect on Drinking Water;" "Trade Nuisances;" "Common Adulterations of Foods;" " Fevers and Infectious Diseases ; How they are Warded Off by Sanitation ;" "Filtration of Sewage through Coal;" "Safeguarding and Examination of Public Water Supplies;" "Reports on Health of County of Warwick," 1889-1902. Contrib. "Condensed Milk," *Birm. Med. Rev.*1884; "Diphtheria," *Pub. Health*, 1889; " Milk Scarlatina," *Ibid.* 1891.

HILL, CHARLES ALEX., 13, Rodney-st. Liverpool—M.B.,B.C.Camb.1893,B.A.(Honours Nat.Sc.Tripos)1889; M.R.C.S., L.R.C.P.Lond.1893; D.P.H. Vict. 1900; (*Camb.* and *St. Geo.*); Asst. Phys. Liverp. Hosp. for Consump. and Dis. of Chest; Hon. Bacteriol. David Lewis North. Hosp.; Med. Ref. Gresh. and other Assur.Cos.; Mem. Brit. Med. Assoc. and Liverp. Med. Inst.; late Asst. Bacteriol. Roy. Commiss. on Sewage Disposal; Obst. Asst., House Phys., House Surg., Ophth. and Orthop. Asst., and Asst. Surg. Regist. St. Geo. Hosp., and Surg. R.M.S. "Britannic." Contrib. " Bacteriological Report on Case of Puerperal Septicæmia "(with Dr. Raw), *Lancet*, 1898; "Colicystitis as a Complication of Enteric Fever," *Liverp. Med. Chir. Journ.* 1898 ; "The Disinfection of the Excreta" (with Dr. J. H. Abram), *Brit. Med. Journ.* 1898; "A Classification of the Micro-Organisms found in Water" (with Prof. Boyce), *Journ. of Path. and Bacteriol.* 1899 ; " Bile-Salt Broth" (with Dr. A. T. MacConkey), *Thompson-Yates Laborat. Reps.* 1901.

*HILL, CHAS.HAMOR, Cintra, Queen's-rd. St.Heliers, Jersey (retired)—M.D. Brux. 1876 ; M.R.C.S. Eng. and L.S.A.1871;(*St.Bart.*);late Res.Accouch.St. Bart. Hosp., and House Surg. St. Mark's Hosp.

*HILL, EDWD. BRERETON (*Travelling*)—B.A. Camb. 1883, M.B., B.C. 1893; M.R.C.S. Eng. and L.S.A. 1887 ; (*Camb.* and *St. Thos.*); Mem. Brit. Med. Assoc.; late Med. Off. Roy. Hosp. Richmond and House Surg. Gen. Hosp. Birm. Author of "Headache in Children and its Causes" (Thesis). Contrib. "A Fatal Case of Mussel Poisoning," *Brit. Med. Journ.* 1895.

HILL, EDWD. FALKNER, 1, High-st. Chorlton-on-Medlock, Manchester—M.B., Ch.B. Vict.1900; M.R.C.S., L.R.C.P. Lond. 1900; (*Owens Coll.*); late Res. Med. Off.

Entry for Thomas Frederic Higgs in the 1904 Medical Directory. (Courtesy of Familyrelatives.com) then in Dudley, Worcestershire up to 1875. Thereafter, the *Register* lists Edward as being 'Near Inverell, New South Wales' until his death in 1907.

Although it is true that Edward was a house surgeon and administrator of chloroform at St Bartholomew's Hospital and, later, a general practitioner in Dudley and an honorary surgeon at the town's Guest Hospital, his whereabouts given in the *Register* after 1874 onwards are incorrect. By July 1874, Edward had emigrated with his wife to New South Wales, Australia, where he was a medical officer at Carcoar Hospital and a government medical officer and public vaccinator for the town. From Carcoar, he moved to Cowra in 1885, where he fulfilled the same roles of government medical officer and public vaccinator, before building a private hospital near his home in Darling Street, Cowra. Edward was mayor of the town in both 1889 and 1890. His only son died in 1889.

There is no record for Edward in the Australian medical registers from 1892 onwards – the year his father died, leaving an estate valued at more than £150,000. It is believed that Edward returned to England with his wife in that year to claim his inheritance.

It appears that Edward gave more up-to-date information to the *Medical Directory* than the *Medical Register* in the later years of his life. Between 1893 and 1898, he is listed in the 'Practitioners Resident Abroad' section, in the first year at Inverell, New South Wales, and then at Cowra in the same state. This information is still inaccurate. Edward is not listed at all in the 1899 *Medical Directory*, but from 1900 until 1903 he is described as retired and his address was Lyd House, Lydford, Devon. By 1904, his address is given as 'Royal Colonial Institute, Northumberland Avenue, WC' in London, but this may have been a 'holding' address, rather than his residential address. Edward died in Eastbourne in 1907, with an estate valued at £48,201 12s. 6d.

(With thanks to Gloria Hargreave and to Stephen Due of the Australian Medical Pioneers Index for the above information)

The *Medical Register* 1779, 1780 and 1783

For late eighteenth century physicians, surgeons and apothecaries, the *Medical Register* for 1779, 1780 and 1783 can be consulted. Although it was not compulsory to be included in it (unlike the later *Medical Register*), you may be lucky enough to find your ancestor listed. Apart from the 1783 edition, there is no name index and it is arranged alphabetically by county: England first, then Wales, followed by Scotland and Ireland. Towns are listed alphabetically within each county. The names of individuals are given, differentiated between physicians, surgeons and apothecaries, but their full addresses are not shown. There is also a list of surgeons and physicians in the army and the Royal Navy, a foreign list, and a list of deaths.

The printed volumes can be seen at the Wellcome Library and other specialist libraries. They are also available as part of the Eighteenth Century Collections Online (ECCO) subscription resource (www.gale.cengage.com/EighteenthCentury). You can view this for free if you are a member of an institution which subscribes to it, for example, a large reference library, the Wellcome Library etc.

The Society of Apothecaries' printed lists of licentiates

Under the Apothecaries Act of 1815, licentiateships of the Society of Apothecaries could be granted to medical professionals who had undergone a course of training. The resulting qualification was the LSA (Licentiateship of the Society of Apothecaries), which was granted to practitioners in the provinces as well as London. If your ancestor was in general practice, it is highly likely that he or she held a licentiateship.

There is a printed list of licentiates of the Society of Apothecaries from 1815. It can be seen at the Wellcome Library, the Guildhall Library and it may be available at other large reference libraries. It is arranged in alphabetical order, giving the date of qualification and place of residence. This is a useful source if your ancestor was no longer practising medicine after 1845 when the first *Medical Directory* was published. The information can be used to supplement details obtained from trade directories.

Some medical professionals who were already in general practice before the Act also applied for the society's licentiateship in 1815, so it's worth checking if your ancestor was practising in the early nineteenth century.

After the Medical Act of 1886, the society's diploma was altered to cover medicine, surgery and midwifery. The new law specified that students qualifying to practise medicine also had to be examined in surgery. A printed list of licentiates who attained this qualification is available from 1887 onwards. From 1907, the LSA was changed to LMSSA (Licence in Medicine and Surgery of the Society of Apothecaries).

University printed lists

The information gleaned from the *Medical Register* or *Medical Directory* can help you to identify which university your ancestor studied at. Many of the main universities have produced printed volumes listing their graduates. including Oxford, Cambridge, London, Durham, Edinburgh, Glasgow, St Andrews and Aberdeen. These printed lists can be seen at the Wellcome Library, the Guildhall Library or they may be available in other large reference libraries.

Records of the Royal College of Surgeons of Edinburgh

With a charter dating back to 1505, the Royal College of Surgeons of Edinburgh is one of the oldest medical incorporations in the world. It started life as the Incorporation of Barbers and Surgeons of Edinburgh and by 1778 it was granted a new charter and incorporated as the Royal College of Surgeons of Edinburgh.

The library of the Royal College of Surgeons of Edinburgh (www.library. rcsed.ac.uk) holds records of membership from 1505 plus listings of licentiateships, honorary fellowships, diplomas and dental fellowships. In addition, there is a database of nearly 37,000 names in the 'Fellows Roll' arranged in order of roll number, with varying amounts of biographical information on each individual listed. Examination records for those who were awarded double and triple qualifications are also available. In addition, the records of the Society of Barbers are held at the library.

Library staff can carry out an archival enquiry on your behalf; a fee is charged for this service (see the website for more information).

Records of the Royal College of Physicians of Edinburgh

The Royal College of Physicians of Edinburgh was founded in 1681. After agreement was reached with the Royal College of Surgeons of Edinburgh, a joint diploma in medicine and surgery was created in 1859. From 1884, the triple diploma was introduced when the two Edinburgh Royal Colleges collaborated with the Royal Faculty of Physicians and Surgeons of Glasgow. The resulting qualification meant that recipients had an extremely long list of letters after their name.

The Royal College of Physicians of Edinburgh introduced 'membership' in 1860 as a halfway stage between licentiate and fellow. The records of fellows are held in the college's library and genealogical enquiries are welcome (www.rcpe.ac.uk/library/services.php).

Records of the Royal College of Physicians and Surgeons of Glasgow

Founded in 1599, this institution was known as the Faculty of Physicians and Surgeons of Glasgow from the end of the seventeenth century until 1909. In that year, the prefix 'Royal' was added to its name, and in 1962 it became the Royal College of Physicians and Surgeons of Glasgow.

The faculty introduced the grade of licentiate from 1785 to allow country practitioners to be admitted, and there is a 'Register of Single Licentiates 1815–1919' in the college archive, as well as registers and printed lists of fellows.

On the college's website, there is a useful fact sheet about tracing doctors (www.rcpsg.ac.uk/FellowsandMembers/libraryservices).

A GP in his surgery, 1920s. (Author's collection)

Records of the Royal College of Physicians of London

Established in 1518, the Royal College of Physicians of London was granted the power to license those qualified to practise medicine in the capital (extended to the whole of England in 1523). From around the 1880s, the most popular qualification for those wanting to go into general practice was the so-called 'conjoint': the Licentiate of the Royal College of Physicians (LRCP) and the Member of the Royal College of Surgeons of England (MRCS). It's worth remembering that the College of General Practitioners (later Royal College of General Practitioners) was not founded until 1952.

The college has a dedicated heritage centre with a wealth of material relating to physicians (www.rcplondon.ac.uk). One of the most valuable resources is William Munk's *Roll of the Royal College of Physicians of London*. Eleven printed volumes of this biographical directory are available: Volumes 1–3 cover 1518–1825, including both fellows and licentiates, while Volume 4 onwards (from 1826) only includes fellows. They can be consulted in the heritage centre, as well as at the Wellcome Library and other archives and city libraries.

There is a searchable online index to the printed entries (www.rcplondon. ac.uk/heritage/munksroll/munk_index.asp), which will give you the precise page references you need to find your ancestor in the printed volumes.

Records of the Royal College of Surgeons of England

After the surgeons split from the Barber-Surgeons' Company in 1745, the Corporation of Surgeons was set up. This evolved into the Royal College of Surgeons of England, founded in 1800.

The college's library holds a number of records which may be useful for family history research, but only if your ancestor was a fellow of the college in the nineteenth century (not simply a member), or if he practised in London between 1745 and 1800. The library does not have any information for medical professionals who held the MRCS (Member of the Royal College of Surgeons) qualification over and above what is given in the *Medical Register* or *Medical Directory*.

The examination books of the Royal College of Surgeons of England cover the period 1745–1800 and are held at the college's library. They list only the surgeon's name, the date the examination was passed and the town in which he lived. Another useful source is the Corporation of Surgeons' lists spanning the years 1777–99.

Family historians can make an appointment to visit the library on Wednesdays. Alternatively, a research service is available, for which a charge is made; up-to-date details can be found on the website (www.rcseng.ac.uk/library/historicalresearch).

Fellows who died between 1844 and 2002 are listed in the biographical register, *Plarr's Lives of the Fellows of the Royal College of Surgeons of England*. This resource is available in the college's library, at the Wellcome Library and many other archives and large city libraries.

There is also an online version at http://livesonline.rcseng.ac.uk, which is gradually being added to. If you can't find your ancestor listed and you know that he or she was a fellow, there is an index of names for the print editions that you can search – it provides the precise volume and page numbers to find the full entry.

Records of the Royal College of Physicians in Ireland

The Royal College of Physicians in Ireland was founded in 1692. The college's library holds registers which list fellows, honorary fellows, licentiates and members from 1692 to the present day. Of great interest to family historians is the Kirkpatrick Archive, which is an outstanding collection of biographical information on over 10,000 Irish doctors, from earliest times to the mid-twentieth century.

To undertake genealogical research at the library, you should make an appointment or the librarian can carry out a search for you. A charge is made for this service; see the website for more details (www.rcpi.ie/Pages/Library.aspx).

Records of the Royal College of Surgeons in Ireland

The Royal College of Surgeons in Ireland was granted its charter in 1784; in 1844, a supplemental royal charter enabled it to divide its graduates into licentiates and fellows.

The library of the Royal College of Physicians of Ireland offers a genealogical service which includes alumni of the Royal College of Surgeons in Ireland (see above).

Records of the Worshipful Society of Apothecaries of London

In 1617, the Society of Apothecaries was incorporated as a City Livery Company by royal charter from James I. This meant that anyone practising the skill of compounding and dispensing medicines within the City of London and within a seven-mile radius of it had to be members of the society. By the early nineteenth century, apothecaries had developed into doctors offering advice and dispensing their own medicines – akin to today's general practitioners.

Surviving records which can be helpful to family historians include registers of apprenticeship bindings 1694–1836; registers of freedom admissions 1674–80 and 1694–1890 (membership of the society as freemen); and quarterage books 1667–1883 (recording quarterly membership dues). However, it is important to realise that unless your apothecary ancestor was a freeman of the society or was apprenticed to a member, he will not be recorded. Also, if your apothecary was practising between 1617 and 1815 and he lived outside London, there will be no record of him at the Society of Apothecaries.

The London Metropolitan Archives holds microfilmed copies of these records for the Society of Apothecaries (www.lma.gov.uk). Licentiateship registers 1815–87 and candidates' qualification entry books 1815–88 are also held. These microfilms can be viewed at the Guildhall Library.

Records of the Barber-Surgeons' Company of London

The Barber-Surgeons' Company of London was founded in 1540 as a City Livery Company. Until 1745, both barbers and surgeons belonged to the company, hence the name. Anyone practising as a barber or surgeon within the City of London or a seven-mile radius of it had to be a member of the company.

The company's registers of apprentice bindings 1657–1786 and registers of freedom admissions 1522–1801 are extremely useful for family historians. However, only barber-surgeons practising in the City of London may be found in these records. No-one practising in the provinces will be recorded. The London Metropolitan Archives holds microfilmed copies of membership and apprenticeship records for the Barber-Surgeons' Company (www.lma.gov.uk).

From 1745, the surgeons split from the barber-surgeons and set up their own Company of Surgeons, which became the Royal College of Surgeons in 1800. The Barber-Surgeons' Company became the Barbers' Company, and if your surgeon ancestor was apprenticed after 1745, it is unlikely he will be in the Barbers' Company records.

Medical college training records

If your ancestor trained for a medical career in the nineteenth century or later, it may be possible to find records of his or her medical college training. Your first step should be to check the city in which your ancestor studied from the entries in the *Medical Register* or *Medical Directory*. The types of records available may include: entrance papers; attendance registers; report books; prize lists and examination results; and student fees books.

Medical college records can also be a good source of information about the staff who taught the students, as personnel files and salaries/wages books may have survived. Bear in mind that in the majority of cases, staff and student files are closed for eighty years from the last date on the file.

For London-trained doctors, there is an excellent family history guide on the King's College Archives website at www.kcl.ac.uk/archives, which lists in detail the records that are available for King's College Hospital and Medical School, Guy's Hospital and Medical School, and St Thomas's Hospital and Medical School. While some of these records are held at London Metropolitan Archives or other repositories, the guide provides a useful starting point.

You may be able to find the locations of records for other London medical colleges by searching on A2A (www.a2a.org.uk) or AIM25 (www.aim25.ac.uk). For medical training colleges in the provinces, try searching A2A using the 'advanced search' option and entering the institution's name in the 'exact wording or phrase' box. The A2A database contains catalogues describing archives held locally in England and Wales.

For Scottish medical training colleges, you can search for available records on the Scottish Archive Network website (www.scan.org.uk). Collections may be in the individual university's 'special collections' archives, or with one of the royal colleges, particularly for private medical schools. For instance, the Royal College of Physicians and Surgeons of Glasgow holds a number of records relating to medical colleges in the city, including Anderson's College and Portland Street Medical School.

Hospital records

If you've discovered that your ancestor worked in a specific hospital, the next step should be to find out if staff records still exist. You can do this by searching the Hospital Records Database (www.nationalarchives.gov.uk/hospitalrecords), and keying in either the name of the hospital or the town. Bear in mind that hospital names changed over time. Click on the entry for the hospital you're interested in, then scroll down to the bottom where the available records are listed in order of type. You're specifically looking for staff records, and if there are any, the database will name the archive or library where the records are held.

You can then find out more about the exact nature of the records by searching on A2A (www.a2a.org.uk). Enter the name of the archive and the hospital. This should give an indication of the type of staff records available, as well as the years they cover. If no records are found, try looking on the archive's own website in case some of their catalogue is not listed on A2A. Many archives have very comprehensive online catalogues.

Where records still exist, registers of staff can record the date of appointment, the post to which he/she was appointed, and the date of leaving. Sometimes, salaries are also noted, as well as the previous place of work.

General minutes of the hospital board are also valuable as they can include information about interviewing candidates for vacant appointments and who was successful, as well as holiday requests, complaints about standards of work, accommodation or treatment of patients by staff. The annual reports issued by hospitals for their subscribers list the names of their key staff at the front, so it's worth checking these as well.

Medical and surgical committee minute books can also give an insight into your ancestor's working life, and may even include their comments. If patient records survive and your ancestor was a physician or surgeon who treated them, you may even see his or her own handwriting or notes.

Ecclesiastical licences

Medical practitioners in England and Wales could be licensed by one of a number of different authorities, including the bishop of the diocese in which they worked. If your ancestor was practising medicine between 1511 and the late eighteenth century, it's worth checking to see if a licence exists for him. You can check A2A (www.a2A.org.uk) to see what records are available by keying in 'medical licence'.

There is a very helpful research guide to the medical licences issued by the Archbishop of Canterbury between 1535 and 1775 on the Lambeth Palace Library website (www.lambethpalacelibrary.org/content/medicallicences). It includes sample entries, a place index and a name index.

The Wellcome Library has a number of printed sources about ecclesiastical licences, including extracts from those for the Gloucester and Hereford Consistory Courts, compiled by A W J Haggis (http://library.wellcome.ac.uk).

Medical Practitioners in the Diocese of London 1529–1725 by J H Bloom and
   R R James (1935)
A Dictionary of English Country Physicians 1603–1643 by John H Raach
   (1962)

The above printed volumes are useful sources to check if your ancestor was
practising in the sixteenth or seventeenth centuries.

Eighteenth Century Medics by P J and R V Wallis (1988)

This impressive reference work contains the details of around 35,000 medical
practitioners who were active in the eighteenth century. The information was
taken from a number of different sources, including apprenticeship papers,
licences, university alumni lists and book subscriptions. It can be consulted at
the Wellcome Library and many large reference libraries and specialist archives.

The list is arranged alphabetically by surname and individuals are coded
with particular letters: 'M' for master, 'A' for apprentice, 'P' for parent, 'BIL' for
bishop's licence, 'SUB' for a subscriber to medical books and 'SSS' for
significant subscribers. An individual can appear more than once – for instance,
first when he was an apprentice, and later when he himself was a master with
an apprentice of his own. The names denoted by the letter 'P' refer to the parent
who signed the indenture, useful for determining family relationships.

Professional journals

As doctors became established in their careers, they inevitably developed
specialisms or particular interests. Such areas of interest could be expressed
in the form of articles written for the medical journals of the day, for example,
the *Lancet* or the *British Medical Journal*. Some of these journals are indexed,
so it's well worth checking for your own ancestor; see the general sources
section (Chapter 11) for details.

Poor Law service

If a medical practitioner supplemented his income with a post as a Poor Law
medical officer, his appointment will be recorded in the minutes of the board
of guardians for the union in which he worked, as well as in correspondence
to the Poor Law Board in London. The main series of correspondence
between the central Poor Law Commission or Board and the local Poor Law

authorities is at the National Archives in MH 12. You can find out from A2A whether Poor Law records still exist for the area you're interested in (www.a2a.org.uk). For Scotland, try searching the Scottish Archive Network (www.scan.org.uk) to find out what records are available.

Prison records

The records of prison staff are much more difficult to find than those for the prisoners and convicts they cared for. Where they survive, references may be found to prison medical officers in surgeons' journals and staff registers. Try the A2A database (www.a2a.org.uk) or the Scottish Archive Network (www.scan.org.uk).

Supplementary work

If your medical ancestor worked for friendly societies or sick clubs as a medical officer of health, or as a police surgeon, it may be possible to find out more about their appointment, if the records still exist. The best way to find out is to key in the institution's, police force's or local authority's name into the A2A database (www.a2a.org.uk), using the 'advanced search' option, or try the Scottish Archive Network (www.scan.org.uk).

A medical examination in school, 1913. (Author's collection)

Chapter 13

SOURCES FOR MILITARY MEDICAL OFFICERS

The British Army

The Army List

When tracing an army medical officer, check the *Army List* first. Published annually from 1754 until 1879, and then quarterly until 1922, the official *Army List* provides useful details about each officer, including full name, the different ranks held (starting with the lowest), dates of promotion, number of years of service, whether on full or half-pay, and which regiment he served with. There is an alphabetical index at the back and a subject index, which includes the medical department. From 1881, if you see a small superscript number, like this [22] after your ancestor's name, it refers to a footnote at the end of the list, which usually gives information about war service.

The quarterly *Army List* was replaced by a half-yearly series in 1922. A complete set of the *Army List* is held at the National Archives and other less complete series may be found at large reference libraries. A monthly *Army List* was also published between 1798 until 1940, but it is not indexed until 1867. This includes officers of colonial, militia and territorial units.

The two-volume *Commissioned Officers in the Medical Services of the British Army* by Peterkin, Johnston and Drew (1968) was compiled partly from information in the *Army List*. Volume 1 covers 1660–1898, while Volume 2 covers 1898–1960. The second volume does not include those medical professionals who joined the Royal Army Medical Corps on a temporary commission during the two world wars, since they are not included in the original *Army List*.

From 1839 to 1915, *Hart's Army List* was published in addition to the official *Army List*; this is a useful source because it contains details of war service, which the official *Army List* did not provide until 1881.

Records of Officers of the British Army

The National Archives holds service records for officers of the British Army. They fall into two categories: those from the War Office (WO 25) and those from individual regiments (WO 76). There is a useful research guide, entitled 'British Army: Officers' Records 1660–1913' on the National Archives website at www.nationalarchives.gov.uk/catalogue/RdLeaflet.asp?sLeafletID=13.

Indexed records of regimental surgeons and assistant surgeons between 1790 and 1847 are catalogued under WO 25/3898. They are useful because they include a 'Statement of Home and Foreign Service' completed by each surgeon, providing details of date of birth and war service.

If your ancestor was an army surgeon between 1800 and 1840, try the indexed records of professional education under WO 25/3904–3911. Each surgeon listed the names of the hospitals in which he had studied, together with the classes he attended and degrees or diplomas he had attained. Information about army service on full or half-pay is also included.

The application forms that candidates for commissions as surgeons completed survive for the period 1825–67. They are indexed and catalogued under WO 25/3923–3943. Similar information to that in the records of professional education is provided.

Records which are simply classified as 'officers' records' can also be useful, although they are not specific to medical officers. They include the regimental records of serving officers for 1764–c.1915, catalogued under WO 76. These give details of ranks held, age, marriage and children. You could also try the reports of officers' marriages from 1799–1882, indexed up to 1851 by the wife's maiden name, providing details of place and date of birth and marriage, plus names of witnesses. This series is catalogued under WO 25/3239. There is a single card index to the above series of records for officers' and officers' families at the National Archives in Kew.

There is also a series of baptismal certificates for officers for 1777–1868 in WO 32/8903–8920 and for 1755–1908 in WO 42, with index books for both. The latter has certificates relating to marriages, the birth of children, death and burial.

Indexed registers of the annual bounty paid to officers' widows can also be helpful. They cover the period 1755–1856 and can be found in WO 25/3995. The series PMG 3 to PMG 14 also contains details about retired officers and their widows.

An unidentified Royal Army Medical Corps soldier, c.1915. (Author's collection)

Records of the Company (later Royal College) of Surgeons, London

The Wellcome Library holds certificates for the appointment of army surgeons and surgeons' mates for the period 1787–1826, awarded by the Company (later Royal College) of Surgeons of London. They are catalogued under MSS.5756–76.

Royal Army Medical Corps (RAMC) records

The service records for officers of the Royal Army Medical Corps who received permanent commissions between 1871 and 1922 are held at the National Archives. They can be accessed via the index in WO 338/23, and are listed in WO 339. Unfortunately, the service records of surgeons and physicians who joined the RAMC as temporary officers during the First World War were destroyed after 1920.

The records for RAMC officers serving after 1922 are held by the Army Personnel Centre. They can only be accessed by proven next-of-kin; more details are available on the website (www.army.mod.uk/welfare-support/family/6980.aspx).

The Wellcome Library holds the RAMC muniment collection, consisting of diaries, photographs and other writings by individual personnel. They can help to build up a picture of what life was like in the RAMC.

The Royal Navy

The Navy List

This printed source began life in 1782 as *Steel's Navy List* and was published quarterly from 1814. It lists officers serving in the Royal Navy; from 1793, surgeons are included in most of the volumes, in order of seniority: surgeons, staff surgeons and fleet surgeons.

There is a subject index at the front which includes medical officers, an alphabetical list of active officers, and a retired list for those who were no longer serving. Both indexes refer to the medical officers section, in which men are listed in order of the year they joined the service. Officers on the retired list are shown in italics. If there is a number before the person's name, this denotes the ship on which they were serving at the time.

The *Navy List* is widely available at the National Archives, the Society of Genealogists, and most large reference libraries. The unofficial *New Navy List*, published from 1841 to 1856, contains useful potted biographies, so it's worth looking at if your ancestor was serving during this time period.

A list of His Majesty's ships ... of the Royal Navy: to which is added, a list of the captains, lieutenants, masters and commanders. Also a list of the principal officers of His Majesty's land forces, 1741

This source is useful for finding surgeons who were in the Royal Navy before the *Navy List* was established. It can be seen at the Wellcome Library and may be available at other large reference libraries.

O'Byrne's Naval Biographical Dictionary

This is another valuable printed source listing naval officers in 1849, arranged alphabetically by surname.

Records of the Royal Navy

The National Archives holds a number of Royal Navy records that can be useful for tracing medical staff. In the first instance, check the guide entitled 'Royal Navy: Officers' Service Records', which can be seen on the National Archives website (www.nationalarchives.gov.uk/catalogue/RdLeaflet.asp?s LeafletID=287).

The service registers for Royal Navy officers are available on microfilm for the period 1774–1966, and there is also a partial name index. The main series is catalogued under ADM 196, but most entries cover 1840–1920. The details given include dates and places of birth and death, home address, name of wife and date of marriage, plus the names of the ships on which the officer served.

You can also try the 'Returns of Officers' Service' for 1817 and 1846 if your ancestor was serving at this time. Catalogued under ADM 9, they are incomplete because many officers did not return their forms.

The National Archives also holds officers' passing certificates, including a section specifically for surgeons for 1700–1800, which is catalogued under ADM 106. There is also a card index to this series of certificates in the Research Enquiries Room at Kew.

Full and half-pay registers can also be searched for your ancestor for the period 1697–1924. They are catalogued in the series ADM 22–ADM 25, as well as PMG 15. Although half-pay was a retainer for officers, unofficially it was also a form of pension.

Some of the available records can be used to trace wives and next of kin. These include a series of marriage certificates submitted between 1866 and 1902, catalogued under ADM 13/70–71 and ADM 13/186–192. It's also worth trying the series of pension records relating to officers' widows, which can be found under ADM 7/809–814, ADM 22, ADM 23, PMG 16, PMG 19 and PMG 20.

The Naval Medal Rolls are also held at the National Archives under ADM 171. Covering the period from 1793 to 1975, they include: the Naval General Service Medal 1793–1840; the Crimea Medal 1854–55; the British War Medal and the Victory Medal awarded during the First World War.

In addition, the National Archives holds over a thousand journals of medical officers in the Royal Navy, catalogued under ADM 101. They span the years 1793–1880 and give a good indication of the conditions in which medical officers were working, as well as events that happened on particular voyages.

If your naval medical officer worked during the period covered by the journals, you can search the catalogue for his name (www.nationalarchives.gov.uk/catalogue). Enhanced entries are being uploaded to the catalogue on an ongoing basis.

Barber-Surgeons' Company certificates

Anyone wishing to become a navy surgeon had to be examined by, and receive certificates from, the Barber-Surgeons' Company – or, after 1745, from its successor bodies, the Company of Surgeons and the Royal College of Surgeons. The London Metropolitan Archives holds records of certificates issued between 1705 and 1745, which includes surgeons from the provinces as well as London. These certificates are catalogued under Ms 05264.

The Honourable East India Company

The records of the Honourable East India Company and the Indian Army (1861–1947) are in the India Office Records collection at the British Library. There is a very useful online database of more than 300,000 births, baptisms, burials and marriages from the India Office Records collection (http://indiafamily.bl.uk/UI/). This includes the medical staff of the Honourable East India Company, and you can search using names, dates and places.

The database originated as a card index in the 1970s and, although it is a very good starting point, probably less than 10 per cent of the biographical sources available were incorporated into the index.

Specific original records in the British Library, relating to East India Company surgeons, include appointments before 1804, which are recorded across a number of different series: court minutes (B series), committee of correspondence records (D series) general correspondence (E series), factory records (G series) and proceedings (P series).

For the indentures of appointments of surgeons serving between 1771 and 1827, try the bonds and agreements section in the biographical series (O/1/1-79). There are also assistant surgeons' and surgeons' papers for the period 1804–1914 (L/MIL/9/358–408, L/MIL/9/413–427), and there is an index (Z/L/MIL/9/5) in the Asian and African Studies Reading Room.

A Biographical Index of East India Company Maritime Service Officers 1600–1834 *by Anthony Farrington (1999)*

Surgeons serving onboard ship with the East India Company between 1800 and 1834 are listed in this useful printed source. It is available at the Guildhall Library and many other reference libraries.

The Indian Army and Medical Service

An Alphabetical List of the Medical Officers of the Indian Army 1764–1838 *by Edward Dodwell and James S Miles*

Published in 1839, this volume covers the three 'presidencies' of Bengal, Madras and Bombay, plus Prince of Wales Island. It includes the full name, dates of appointments and promotions, and date of death for each officer listed. The date of death is listed even if it did not take place in the United Kingdom or India.

The East India Register *1808–1844*

This index consists of returns of births, marriages and deaths from 1807, and it can be seen at the British Library in the India Office Records collection. Extracts from original volumes are being added regularly.

Indian Army and Civil Service List 1861–1876

This is another useful source in the British Library, which lists departmental and warrant officers of the East India Company's armies and the Indian Army.

Roll of the Indian Medical Service 1615–1930 *by D G Crawford (1930)*

This useful printed volume includes the date of birth, medical qualifications, appointments, promotions, military campaigns, medals and date of death for every individual listed.

Chapter 14

SOURCES FOR OTHER MEDICAL PROFESSIONALS

Anaesthetists

The Association of Anaesthetists of Great Britain and Ireland was founded in 1932. Its museum, archives and library is housed in the Anaesthesia Heritage Centre.

In the archives, there are annual reports for the period 1933–99 (with gaps), which include lists of members up to 1969. There are also a number of records relating to membership of the association, as well as an undated album of

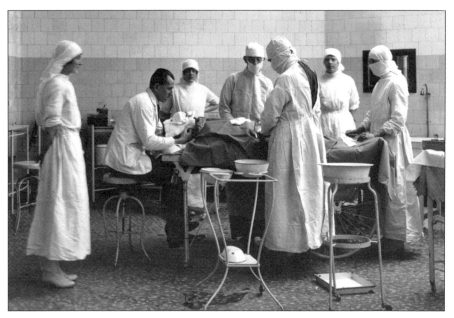

An anaesthetic (chloroform or ether) being administered via the mask and gauze method, c.1905. (Courtesy of Dr Ian Paterson, Department of Anaesthesia, Northern General Hospital, Sheffield)

photographs and biographies of officers. If your ancestor was a president of the association, more documents will be available, including an album of photographs and obituaries of presidents between 1932 and 2002. More details about available records can be found on the association's website (http://aagbi.org).

Dentists

The Medical Directory

You may find your ancestor in the *Medical Directory* (not the *Medical Register*) if he or she was a qualified dentist between 1866 and 1924. During these years, it printed lists of licentiates and graduates in dental surgery, giving full name, address, qualification and where the dentist was working or had worked. Like the entries for qualified doctors, they also provide details of any publications or papers that the dentist had written, or the professional societies he or she was a member of.

The Dentists' Register *(from 1879)*

Like the *Medical Register*, the *Dentists' Register*, which began in 1879, does not provide as much information as the *Medical Directory*. The details given include full name and address, the date of registration and the name of the qualification and where it was obtained. It is still worth checking to trace your ancestor's career, year on year, especially for changes of address. Dental practitioners who could prove they had been in practice in dentistry before 1879, either specialising in dentistry or combined with medicine, surgery or pharmacy, were also included on the register.

If you cannot find your ancestor listed, but you know that he or she worked as a dentist, it just means he or she was not formally qualified. Many highly skilled, successful practitioners saw no need to be listed on the register and could practise in 'dental rooms' as long as they did not describe themselves as a 'dentist' or 'dental surgeon'. They may also have been members of rival associations, such as the Incorporated Society of Extractors and Adaptors of Teeth Ltd. It was only after the 1921 Dentists Act was passed that this loophole was closed.

The British Dental Association museum holds copies of the *Dentists' Register* and you can check it, along with other sources, in return for a donation. There is a very useful page on the website about dentist ancestors (www.bda.org/museum/enquiries/was-ancestor-dentist.aspx). The BDA museum also holds copies of dental journals such as the *British Journal of Dental Science*, which may include an obituary for your ancestor, and even advertising of his or her services. You could also try trade directories (see the General Sources section).

Medical and Dental Students' Register: Lists of Medical and Dental Students Registered During the Year *(1911–37)*

If your ancestor qualified between 1911 and 1937, the Wellcome Library has a printed volume, compiled for the General Medical Council, which lists all medical and dental students registered between these dates.

Royal College of Physicians and Surgeons of Glasgow

Examination registers for dentists who qualified for the Licentiate in Dental Surgery in Glasgow are in the archives of the Royal College of Physicians and

The east filling room at Birmingham's Dental School, 1906. (Courtesy of the School of Dentistry, Birmingham)

Surgeons of Glasgow. The registers cover the period between 1879 and 1961. More information can be found on the website (www.rcpsg.ac.uk/Fellows andMembers/ArchiveServices/Pages/mem_spdentarchives.aspx).

Brass Plate and Brazen Impudence: Dental Practice in the Provinces 1755–1855 by Christine Hillam (1991)

If your dentist ancestor practised in the provinces in the mid-eighteenth and nineteenth centuries, it's worth checking this invaluable printed source. It contains entries for dentists taken from a survey of all provincial trade directories up to 1855. The appendices also include biographical information about many of the dentists listed.

Gynaecologists

The Royal College of Obstetricians and Gynaecologists (RCOG) was not founded until 1929. Before this date, it is difficult to find specific information about gynaecologists, other than in the usual medical directories and journals.

Membership records

Fellows of the college could put the initials FRCOG after their name, while members could use the nomenclature MRCOG. The printed source *The Lives of the Fellows of the Royal College of Obstetricians and Gynaecologists 1929–1969* by John Peel (1976) is a good starting point. It contains biographical information about fellows of the college only, and is available at the Wellcome Library and other large reference libraries. If your ancestor was a member and not a fellow, he or she will not be listed.

However, the RCOG archives holds an alphabetical list of founder fellows and members from the first annual report (1929–30); a copy from the fifth annual report for 1934–35 is also available. Annual reports for the years 1932–33, 1939–44, 1948 and 1950–2007 can be consulted, which contain obituaries and details of new fellows and members. Also in the archives are card indexes of deceased and living FRCOG and MRCOG holders between 1929 and 1998, which include the date of admission to the fellowship or membership of the college.

Journals

The *Journal of Obstetrics and Gynaecology of the British Empire* was first published in 1902. It later became the *Journal of Obstetrics and Gynaecology of the British Commonwealth*, and then from 1975, *British Journal of Obstetrics and Gynaecology*. Its current title is *BJOG: An International Journal of Obstetrics and Gynaecology*. The RCOG archives hold an almost complete run of the journal from 1923 onwards, and it can be useful for finding out more about your ancestor's working life and the issues of the day, as well as a source of obituaries.

Other sources

Another useful source is the large collection of photographs of past presidents, fellows and members and other eminent gynaecologists and obstetricians. The archives also hold the papers of gynaecological member clubs, which, in some cases, pre-date the founding of the college. The RCOG archive catalogue can be viewed online through the AIM25 website (www.aim25.ac.uk).

Opticians

British Optical Association records

The British Optical Association museum holds the BOA register for 1895–1962 and BOA yearbooks for 1914, 1927, 1930, 1938, 1951 and 1960. These volumes include the names of members of the association, who were usually qualified ophthalmic opticians, but there are also some dispensing associates, student members and overseas members in the lists. Another useful source is the BOA Register of Candidates for Examination, 1895–*c*.1940s.

Other registers

The museum also has copies of the Institute of Ophthalmic Opticians' membership book for 1927; the 'Blue Book of Opticians' for 1939; the National Association of Opticians Register 1955–56; and various registers for the Scottish Association of Opticians, the Institute of Chemist Opticians, the Institute of Ophthalmic Opticians, the Institute of Optical Science and the Contact Lens Society.

General Optical Council membership records

For more recent ancestors, the General Optical Council *Opticians Register* (1960–2005) can be consulted.

Journals

Obituaries of your ancestor may be found in *The Optician* (1891–present), *The Refractionist* (pre-1924–40), the *National Optical Journal* (1933–51), *The Ophthalmic Optician* (1961–84), *Optometry Today* (1985–present), and the *Dioptric Review* (1895–1953, followed by *Dioptric News* until 1960).

Staff at the British Optical Association museum can carry out a free search of the available records; a fee is charged for photocopies and scanned images. Check the website for more details (www.college-optometrists.org).

Pharmacists, chemists and druggists

Before 1841, there was no professional body for pharmacists, chemists or druggists. Prior to this time, the only sources listing them are trade directories (see the General Sources section).

Pharmaceutical Journal

The weekly *Pharmaceutical Journal*, published by the Royal Pharmaceutical Society of Great Britain from 1841, contains listings of members, associates and those who had passed its examinations. As it was not compulsory to register with the society prior to 1868, the lists of members and associates are incomplete before this time. Early members and associates tended to be from the London area. The first 'Register of Pharmaceutical Chemists' was established under the 1852 Pharmacy Act. It was not published, but some of its details appeared in the journal's lists. It included those who were members of the society before 1852, those proprietors who opted to take the last opportunity to become members without qualifying, and those who had passed the major examination.

The *Pharmaceutical Journal* also includes obituaries of more prominent members, and the library of the Royal Pharmaceutical Society of Great Britain holds copies of the journal from when it began.

The **Annual Register of Pharmaceutical Chemists** *and the* **Annual Register of Chemists and Druggists** *(from 1868)*

From 1868, it became compulsory for anyone dealing in or compounding medicines containing poisons to register with the Pharmaceutical Society before being able to practise. Two annual registers were kept and published: one for chemists and druggists, and the other for pharmaceutical chemists (the latter was for higher-qualified individuals or those who had a long-established business). Those on the *Register of Pharmaceutical Chemists* were automatically included on the *Register of Chemists and Druggists*.

The registers are arranged in alphabetical order of surname and the information provided includes date of registration, residence, type of examination taken, the certificate number and qualification obtained. No details are given about date of birth, apprenticeship or place of study.

The Royal Pharmaceutical Society holds a complete run of both registers. Its museum offers a special research service to family historians, under which all the relevant registers are checked for details of your ancestor. A basic research fee is charged per person or premises searched (check the website for current details of fees at www.rpsgb.org.uk/informationresources/museum/services/. A very useful resource sheet is provided as part of the service.

The **Register of Premises** *(from 1936)*

If your ancestor was a chemist, druggist or pharmaceutical chemist after 1936, you can also check the Pharmaceutical Society's *Register of Premises*. The register is arranged by place, then alphabetical premises' name within each place, so you will need to know roughly where your ancestor practised. From 1938, entries are included for both proprietor's names and trading names if they are different. Each entry gives the precise address of the premises.

Physiotherapists

The Chartered Society of Physiotherapists (CSP) was originally founded in 1894 as the Society of Trained Masseuses. The CSP Learning Resource Centre holds large numbers of books, pamphlets and journals about the society, some of which may be useful for family history research.

Journals

If your ancestor was an active member of the society – for example, as a founder member, president or committee member – you will have more chance of finding him or her in the available records. You may be able to find an obituary in the society's journal, *Physiotherapy*, which began in 1915. If your ancestor was an ordinary, passive member, it is unlikely that he or she will be mentioned.

Another useful journal is *Nursing Notes*, which included the society's regular massage section. This also included the society's announcements, articles by doctors and senior masseuses, details of training, book reviews and letters.

The CSP Learning Resource Centre is unable to undertake family history enquiries, but visitors are welcome to make an appointment to view the available sources. Check the 'About the CSP' section of the website for more details (www.csp.org.uk).

Membership registers of the Chartered Society of Physiotherapy

The Wellcome Library holds membership registers for the period 1895–1975, plus published lists of members for 1920–86.

Psychiatrists

The Royal College of Psychiatrists was founded in 1841 as the Association of Medical Officers of Asylums and Hospitals for the Insane. It was renamed the Medico-Psychological Association in 1865 and the Medico-Psychological Association of Great Britain and Ireland in 1887. After receiving a royal charter in 1926, it became the Royal Medico-Psychological Association (RMPA). Finally, in 1971, it changed its status to become the Royal College of Psychiatrists.

Journal of Mental Science

The association's journal, the *Journal of Mental Science*, began in 1855 and from the beginning until around the 1960s, it printed lists of its members. Yearbooks dating from the 1930s to the 1960s are another source which lists members.

All material more than thirty years old is open to college fellows and members, and other researchers by appointment – at the discretion of the archivist, on payment of a day charge. The website has up-to-date information about the daily fee (www.rcpsych.ac.uk/members/thecollege archives.aspx).

Asylum annual reports

If you know which asylum your ancestor worked at, you can find out if records still exist for it by checking the Hospital Records Database (www.nationalarchives.gov.uk/hospitalrecords). While some hospitals retain their own archives, in England and Wales, the majority of records have been deposited in county record offices, so you can also check A2A (www.a2a.org.uk). In Scotland, the responsibility for hospital records fell to health boards which have their own archives – they are listed in Appendix 3.

Annual reports were written for the charitable subscribers to each asylum, going into detail about the number of cases treated and discharged. They also list the names of key staff, including the superintendent or medical officer, as well as including a personal statement from the superintendent. This type of document helps to give an idea of the superintendent's personality and his views on treating mental disease.

Radiographers

Although radiography developed quickly in Britain in the 1890s and early 1900s, the Society of Radiographers was not founded until 1920. The archives of the society hold some groups of records that could be useful to family historians. You can read a description of the types of records held on the AIM25 website (www.aim25.ac.uk).

If your ancestor was a member of the society in the 1920s and 1930s, you might find him or her in the membership registers which cover 1921–35. The details include full name and whether the subscription had been paid. The archives also holds printed membership lists for 1929–30, 1933 and 1934; and signed records of receipt of the diploma of membership.

Radiography is the professional journal of the Society of Radiographers. The archives holds copies of the journal from 1935 to the present, in which obituaries and issues of the day can be found.

The archives of the Society of Radiographers is accessible by appointment only. Check the website for the current details of where the archives can be seen (www.sor.org).

Chapter 15

SOURCES FOR CIVILIAN NURSES

Tracing a nurse's career before state registration in 1921 can be difficult, as there was no central register before this date. The only records of nurses appear in the archives of their employers: the hospitals.

Hospital records

If you know your ancestor was a nurse at a specific hospital, records may still exist of her appointment and/or training. You can find out by searching the Hospital Records Database (www.nationalarchives.gov.uk/hospitalrecords) and keying in the town or name of the hospital, and scrolling down to look for staff records. If records survive, the database will tell you where they are held. Bear in mind that records less than seventy-five or fifty years old will be subject to closure, and where a register spans a long period of time, for example from the 1890s until the 1960s, it is at the discretion of the archivist to allow access.

Staff registers of nurses gave broadly the same information across the country. The full names and ages of applicants are listed, together with the name of the person they were recommended by, where they were sent from, and where they went after leaving. The registers can also provide revealing comments about the nurses' characters and abilities. From the 1890s, more detailed probationer registers may also be available, listing the wards in which the probationer or trainee nurse spent her training, together with remarks about her general conduct and abilities.

If you are able to find your ancestor in one of these registers, it's worth cross-checking to see if she is mentioned in the hospital's minute books. At first, appointments of nurses were mentioned in the general or house committee minute books, especially if the post was a senior one, such as a matron or lady superintendent. Towards the end of the nineteenth century, specific nursing committees were set up in hospitals to deal with all aspects of the nursing, including recruiting and appointing. Both committees recorded resignations and dismissals, the advertising of new posts, the awarding of pensions and complaints about staff.

The hospital's annual reports are also a mine of information, recording all the senior staff at the front. If your ancestor was a matron, she should be included in these annual lists.

Records of Nightingale nurses

If you suspect your ancestor trained as a Nightingale nurse at St Thomas's Hospital in London, the records are held at the London Metropolitan Archives (www.lma.gov.uk).

In her chapter entitled 'The Nightingale Nurses: The Myth and the Reality' which appears in Christopher Maggs's book *Nursing History: The State of the Art*, Monica Baly has transcribed what happened to the first 148 Nightingales who trained between 1860 and 1870. The information provided includes registration number, name, age and marital status. It also provides comments about each probationer's health in training and her training report, as well as the appointments she had over the three-year period after qualifying. Some entries include information about the Nightingales' subsequent careers.

Asylum records

Lunatic asylums had to keep similar staff records to hospitals, and they can be tracked down in the same way, by first checking the Hospital Records Database (see above). Registers of staff may include a mixture of trained nurses and untrained asylum attendants.

Poor Law records

As with medical officers, when nurses were appointed to Poor Law institutions, this was recorded in the minutes of the board of guardians for the union in which they worked, and in correspondence to the Poor Law Board in London. The main series of correspondence between the central Poor Law Commission or Board and the local Poor Law authorities is at the National Archives catalogued under MH 12.

As well as appointments, resignations and dismissals, guardians' minute books record all manner of details about their staff, from complaints by inmates and requests for increases in salaries through to problems with living accommodation and holiday dates.

Later in the nineteenth century and into the twentieth, specific registers for staff were set up, including nurses. These volumes increased when it became necessary to provide training for nurses in 1897. The details provided are similar to those for hospital nurses (see above).

You can find out from A2A whether Poor Law records still exist for the area you're interested in (www.a2a.org.uk). For Scotland, try searching the Scottish Archive Network (www.scan.org.uk).

After 1921

Under the terms of the 1919 Nursing Act, the General Nursing Council (GNC) was set up to produce and maintain a register of nurses, and to approve training schools. State registration of nurses started with the founding of the GNC, but the register did not begin until 30 September 1921.

Women who were already nurses had until the end of 1923 to register; this is important because the register contains information about nurses who could have been nursing for thirty or forty years before this date. So if you have a Victorian nurse in your family tree and she was still alive between 1921 and 1923, it's worth checking to see if she's listed. After 1923, only those who had passed state examinations could register.

The Royal College of Nursing has an excellent guide to tracing nurses on its website (www.rcn.org.uk/development/library/archives/factsheets/factsheets-tracingnurses).

Registration records

The **Register of Trained Nurses,** *1891, 1892 and 1896*

The Royal British Nurses' Association, founded in 1887, issued registers of trained nurses who were members of the association. Although numbers were relatively small, the period covered was almost thirty years before state registration. The Wellcome Library has the register for 1891, 1892 and 1896, while King's College London Archives has the 1892 register.

Register of Nurses, 1916–1923

The Royal College of Nursing (RCN) was founded in 1916 as a professional association to represent the interests of nurses, and it later became a union. If you have a nurse in your family tree who was working between 1916 and 1923, you might find her in the published volume issued by the College of Nursing Ltd. It includes full name, the year of joining, address and where trained.

The **Register of Nurses** *(from 30 September 1921)*

First published in 1922, the *Register of Nurses* was issued by the three General Nursing Councils in England and Wales, Scotland and Ireland. It lists nurses alphabetically by surname, their registration date and number, plus their residential address and where, and when, they qualified. The *Register* was produced annually until the late 1940s, after which only new nurses were listed each year, without an address given.

At first, there was a main general section of the register, with supplementary sections for 'fever', 'sick children's', 'male' and 'mental'. If you can't find your ancestor in the general section, try the other sections, as well as the late entries list.

All nurses listed in the general section were State Registered Nurses (SRNs), although the term used in Scotland was Registered General Nurse (RGN). Registration was compulsory after 1943, after which the Assistant or Enrolled Nurse was introduced, later known as the State Enrolled Nurse (SEN).

Registers of nurses for England and Wales can be found at the National Archives, the Wellcome Library and the British Library; and for Scotland at the National Archives of Scotland. The Royal College of Nursing Archives also has incomplete runs of the nursing registers for all three General Nursing Councils (www.rcn.org.uk).

Professional directories

Burdett's Official Nursing Directory was published between 1894 and 1899. It included information about nursing training schools in the UK and abroad and other institutions, plus lists of nurses with their names, addresses and a brief resumé. It was not compulsory to be listed and a fee was charged. Many of the listed nurses were working in London.

Burdett's Hospital Annual was published between 1890 and 1893, and then became *Burdett's Hospital and Charities Annual* from 1894, continuing until 1930. These annuals listed hospitals, institutions, charities and organisations in the UK. It also included the names of senior nursing and medical staff, as well as details about training, the number of nurses on the staff and the size of the hospital.

Journals

Nursing journals are rich sources of information about the changing world of nursing. One of the most valuable sections for family historians is that which lists appointments, retirements, marriages and deaths. You can also find out more about working conditions at the time your ancestor was nursing, issues of the day, and information about pay and pensions.

The RCN Archives has digitised the whole of the *Nursing Record/British Journal of Nursing* on its website (http://rcnarchive.rcn.org.uk). The database is searchable by name or key word, and each issue can also be browsed page by page. The *Nursing Record* was first published in 1888 and it became the *British Journal of Nursing* from 1902.

Chapter 16
SOURCES FOR MILITARY NURSES

I f you're tracing a military nurse, the National Archives has three very useful research guides about nurses in the British Army, the Royal Navy and the Royal Air Force on its website (www.nationalarchives.gov.uk/catalogue).

Army nurses

It can be difficult to find records of early army nurses. From 1886, the *Army List* names the lady nursing superintendents of the Army Nursing Service. For the period 1903–26, the National Archives holds records of the professional qualifications and recommendations for appointments of staff nurses in the Queen Alexandra's Imperial Military Nursing Service (QAIMNS). It is catalogued under WO 25/3956 and is indexed.

If your ancestor served in the Boer War, have a look at Keiron Spires's Boer War Nurses website (www.boerwarnurses.com), which has details of almost 1,000 nurses, plus information about hospitals and hospital ships from the period.

The records of those who served in Voluntary Aid Detachments (VADs) are held at the British Red Cross Archives (www.redcross.org.uk/index.asp?id=3423). Records for those who served in the QAIMNS and in the Territorial Force Nursing Service (TFNS) during the First World War can be found at the National Archives, catalogued under WO 399.

For Second World War service in Queen Alexandra's Royal Army Nursing Corps, the records are held by the Ministry of Defence Army Personnel Centre (see the Useful Contacts section).

Naval nurses

The National Archives holds records of nurses at the Greenwich Naval Hospital between 1704 and 1865, catalogued under ADM 73/83, 73/84, 73/85 and 73/86. These registers provide the name of nurses, date of entry and date and reason for leaving; later entries include details of husbands and children.

An unidentified Red Cross nurse, August 1917. (Author's collection)

It is also the repository for naval nursing records from 1884 onwards, catalogued under ADM 104/43, ADM 104/95 and ADM104/161. The details given for nursing sisters include name, rank, date of birth, date of entry and discharge. Later registers include comments on nurses' characters and abilities.

Royal Air Force nurses

Records of nurses in the Royal Air Force are still held by the RAF Personnel Centre, and can only be provided to proven next-of-kin. A fee is charged for this service (see the Useful Contacts section).

Chapter 17

SOURCES FOR OTHER NURSES

District nurses

The Wellcome Library holds the national roll of the Queen's Nurses Institute for the period 1891–1969, as well as badge registers for good service (1907–45). There is a separate index to the roll, and the collection is catalogued under SA/QNI. The QNI collection contains lots of other records which may be useful for finding out about your ancestor's working life as a district nurse; you can browse the listings of the QNI collection on the Archives and Manuscripts Catalogue (http://library.wellcome.ac.uk/catalogues.html).

At the London headquarters of the Queen's Nursing Institute, there is a wealth of historical material, such as books, papers, photographs, institute records and nursing equipment. These resources can be seen by appointment (www.qni.org.uk). There is a useful index to the resources on the website (www.qni.org.uk/about-us/historical-resources.html).

There may also be surviving records of the regional District Nursing Associations themselves that mention your ancestor's appointment. Try searching on A2A (www.a2a.org.uk) or the Scottish Archive Network (www.scan.org.uk).

Midwives

If your midwife ancestor was practising between the early sixteenth century and the mid-eighteenth century, there may still be a record of a licence issued by the bishops of the diocese in which she worked. The Wellcome Library has a number of sources about ecclesiastical licences, including extracts from those for the Gloucester and Hereford Consistory Courts, compiled by A W J Haggis, and a collection of licences mostly from the Welsh Marches area, 1687–1728 (http://library.wellcome.ac.uk). You can also check A2A (www.a2a.org.uk) to see what records are available by keying in 'midwives' licences'.

A register of midwives examined by the Obstetrical Society of London is held at the National Archives. It covers the period 1872–88 and is catalogued under DV 7/1, although the condition of the register is fragile.

ROLL No. 3778   NAME *Evans, Annie Sarah.*

Reference from Probationers' Register } IV. 39.	Date of Appointment as Queen's Nurse } APR 1 1910
Badge . . . . 1557.	Certificate Awarded *On resignation January 18th 1916, Work & Conduct: Very good*.
Received 1st Gratuity from Benefit Fund }	Leaving Badge granted . . .

Date of Birth . . . . . *July 14th 1878.*	Single or Widow . . . . . *Single.*
Religious Denomination . . *Baptist.*	Occupation of Father . . . *Builder & Contractor.*
Where Educated . . . . . *Bangor.*	How employed before entering Hospital } . . *No occupation.*

Hospital Training *Lambeth Infirmary*   3 *years certificate. February 28th 1904 to July 24th 1909.*

Other Hospital and Nursing Experience

Midwifery Training

District Training *Liverpool Q.V.J.N. Assn. North Home. September 16th 1909 to March 16th 1910.*

* Result :— *Lectures attended. Cookery. Surgery. Hygiene. Social Science. Maternity. Skin diseases.*
Roll Examination. Marks 27. Max. 60. A poor paper, has not been instructed or has not attended to instruction as to Hygiene, etc. All three parts of question 4 attempted.

Other Qualifications and Remarks :—

Cyclist. Speaks Welsh. Helps with Red Cross Work & undertakes Tuberculosis Nursing (June 1914) Undertakes School Nursing & helps with V.A.D. (Dec. 1915)

Superintendent's Report. a good reliable nurse, much appreciated by patients. Inspector's Report. Capable quick worker, suitable for single district.

Entry for Annie Sarah Evans in the Queen's Nursing Institute's Roll of Nurses, 1910–16 – left page. (Courtesy of the Wellcome Library, London)

Entry for Annie Sarah Evans in the Queen's Nursing Institute's Roll of Nurses, 1910–16 – right page. (Courtesy of the Wellcome Library, London)

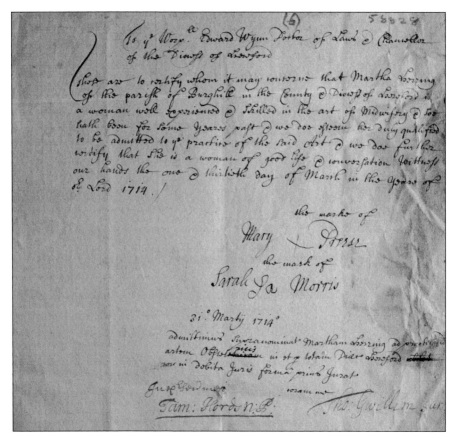

A midwifery certificate for Martha Herring of Burghill, Hereford, dated 31 March 1714.
(Courtesy of the Wellcome Library, London)

The main source for registered midwives is *The Midwives Roll* which began in 1902. The National Archives holds a complete run, while the Wellcome Library has the roll from 1904–59. It may also be available at other large city libraries or archives.

The National Archives also holds case files of the penal board for the Central Midwives Board, 1904–83, which dealt with complaints against midwives on the roll. The files are catalogued under DV 5, but are subject to a seventy-five-year closure period.

Mental nurses

Before 1890, there were no entry examinations for mental nurses or asylum attendants. The Certificate of Proficiency in Mental Nursing was introduced by the Medico-Psychological Association (MPA) in that year, and it remained the only recognised qualification in mental nursing until 1921. There was also a separate Certificate in Mental Deficiency Nursing from 1919 and an Occupational Therapy Certificate from 1939–47.

The archives of the Royal College of Psychiatrists hold registers of successful candidates who took the examinations, which provide full name, the date of examination, place of residence or examination centre, number on register and the names of the supervising doctor. No other personal details, such as date of birth or place of work, are given. Individual volumes are indexed in alphabetical order, but only by the first letter of the alphabet.

The available registers are for the Certificate of Proficiency in Mental Nursing, 1891–1951; Preliminary Examination in Nursing, 1938–49; Certificate of Proficiency in Nursing Mental Defectives, 1919–51; Preliminary Examination in Nursing Mental Defectives, 1938–49; and the Examination in Occupational Therapy, 1939.

All material more than thirty years old is open to college fellows and members, and other researchers by appointment at the discretion of the archivist, on payment of a day charge. The website has up-to-date information about the daily fee (www.rcpsych.ac.uk/members/thecollegearchives.aspx).

Mental nurses are also listed in the *Nursing Register* from 1922. Minute books and correspondence of the association's Scottish division, containing references to training and examinations, are held in Edinburgh University Library (http://www.lib.ed.ac.uk).

Chapter 18

SOURCES FOR PATIENTS

If your ancestor was a hospital or asylum patient, your first port of call should be the Hospital Records Database (www.nationalarchives.gov.uk/hospitalrecords).This lists the location of most surviving hospital records across the UK and is searchable by hospital name or by town. Searching by town is useful because it is common to find that hospital names have changed since their original foundation.

In Scotland, responsibility for hospital records fell to the health boards. These records were sometimes merged into university archives, in other cases records may be held in the archives of the health board for the relevant area. There is a list in the Useful Contacts section.

Hospital records

The coverage of hospital records, especially those relating to patients, can be patchy. If they have survived, the most useful registers for family history are those relating to admission and discharges, as they provide the full name, age and address of patients, together with the date of admission and discharge. More rarely, there may also be medical or surgical registers, which give details about the treatment your ancestor may have received.

If you think your ancestor may have been a patient at one of London's children's hospitals, search the Historic Hospital Admission Records Project database, which covers the Hospital for Sick Children at Great Ormond Street, the Evelina Hospital and the Alexandra Hospital for Children with Hip Disease (http://hharp.org). The database is searchable by name and includes more than 100,000 admission records between 1852 and 1914. Even if your ancestor is not listed, the website provides valuable information about what life was like for children in hospital at this time.

Poor Law records

Workhouses and poorhouses provided hospital treatment for the destitute and those already receiving poor relief. If they have survived, admission and discharge registers are held by county record offices and archives. You can find out what's available by searching A2A (www.a2a.org.uk).

The registers record each individual's full name, the parish to which they were charged, by whose order they were admitted and the reason for seeking relief. Other details include the date of admission, the next meal they were entitled to, and the class for diet. There were nine different classes for diet, including: able-bodied men; old and infirm men; boys from 9 to 13; boys from 2 to 9; able-bodied women; old and infirm women; girls from 9 to 13; girls from 2 to 9; and infants. Inmates were given varying amounts of food according to which dietary class they had been placed in. The registers also record the date and reason for discharge. The age is sometimes given, but not always. Where they survive, other useful records include religious creed registers, punishment books and minutes of the board of guardians, which may include reference to your ancestor if he or she had made a complaint, been apprenticed out, or had been in trouble.

In Scotland, general poor relief registers and applications for poor relief are held in county record offices and archives. Search the Scottish Archive Network (www.scan.org.uk) to find out what's available. Other records which may have survived include separate registers for the able-bodied unemployed, children's registers and claims from other parishes.

Peter Higginbotham's website is an excellent starting point for finding out more about workhouses (http://www.workhouses.org.uk). It allows you to search for specific institutions under 'Workhouse Locations', see old photographs and plans of each one, and find out more about their history.

If you know your ancestor spent time in any of London's workhouses between 1834 and 1940, try searching Ancestry's Poor Law records resource (www.ancestry.co.uk).

Asylum records

For lunatic asylum patients, you can find out what records exist by searching on the Hospital Records Database (see above). This covers both private and public lunatic asylums, which invariably changed their names over the years. Alternatively, you can search on A2A (www.a2a.org.uk) or the Scottish Archive Network (www.scan.org.uk).

Admission and discharge registers may be available, and if you are very lucky, there may also be case books detailing the treatment given to your ancestor. Another type of record was the reception order: if a patient was admitted to an asylum from a workhouse, a reception order had to be completed.

Appendix 1
NURSING TERMINOLOGY

When tracing a nurse in your family tree, it's important to realise that the term 'nurse' could have meant a number of different occupations, and did not necessarily mean the person was qualified or formally trained.

Terms for nurses used in the census

Attendant/ward attendant – male or female member of asylum staff

Charge nurse – similar to ward sister

District nurse – a qualified nurse with additional midwifery training who provided nursing in the community

Hospital nurse – a nurse working in a hospital, not necessarily formally trained unless after 1870s/1880s

Lady probationer – a higher class of woman who paid for her training in nursing

Matron – a woman in charge of all the nursing staff in a hospital

Midwife – someone who had received midwifery training, not necessarily a qualified nurse

Military nurse – a nurse in the British Army, Royal Navy or Royal Air Force

Monthly nurse – someone who looked after a mother and baby in the month after childbirth, also carried out general private nursing

Night nurse – someone who worked the night shift

Private nurse – someone who nursed patients in their own homes, obtaining work through a hospital or agency, or self-employment

Probationer – an unqualified person undertaking training in nursing

Sick nurse – someone who nursed the sick

Sister – often interchangeable with 'hospital nurse' and could refer to any grade

Staff nurse – the starting grade after completing probationer training

Subordinate nurse (sometimes called SMS) – private nurse working through an agency

Superintendent nurse – a grade of hospital nurse who was in charge of particular areas of the hospital, answerable to the matron

Ward sister – a nurse in charge of a ward, senior to staff nurses

'Wet' nurse – a woman who was paid to suckle other women's children

Terms for nurses used after 1922

Nurse or sister tutor – a qualified nurse teacher

Registered fever nurse (RFN or FN) – a qualified nurse who has completed approved training for fever nursing

Registered general nurse (RGN) – a qualified female nurse who has completed approved training for general nursing (a term used in Scotland instead of SRN)

Registered male nurse (not abbreviated to RMN) – a qualified male nurse who has completed approved training for general nursing

Registered mental nurse (RMN) – a qualified nurse who has completed approved training for mental/psychiatric nursing

Registered mental handicap/mentally subnormal nurse – a qualified nurse who has completed approved training for mental handicap or mental subnormality nursing

Registered sick children's nurse (SCN) – a qualified nurse who has completed approved training for sick children's nursing

State enrolled or assistant nurse (SEN) – a qualified nurse at a lower level than SRN/RGN who has completed approved training for enrolled nursing

State registered nurse (SRN) – a qualified female nurse who has completed approved training for general nursing

GLOSSARY OF MEDICAL QUALIFICATIONS

Abbreviations of medical qualifications can be found in the *Medical Register* and the *Medical Directory*, as well as trade directories and the censuses.

Degrees conferred by universities

MD – Doctor of Medicine
MB – Bachelor of Medicine
MC or CM – Master of Surgery
ChB – Bachelor of Surgery
LM – Licentiate in Midwifery
DPH – Diploma of Public Health

Diplomas conferred by chartered colleges

FRCP – Fellow of the Royal College of Physicians
MRCP – Member of the Royal College of Physicians
LRCP – Licentiate of the Royal College of Physicians
FRCPI – Fellow of the Royal College of Physicians (Ireland)
LRCPI – Licentiate of the Royal College of Physicians (Ireland)
FRFPS – Fellow of the Royal Faculty of Physicians and Surgeons (Glasgow)
LRFPS – Licentiate of the Royal Faculty of Physicians and Surgeons (Glasgow)
LM – Licentiate in Midwifery
FRCS – Fellow of the Royal College of Surgeons
MRCS – Member of the Royal College of Surgeons
LRCS – Licentiate of the Royal College of Surgeons

Licences granted by chartered societies and institutions

LSA – Licentiate of the Society of Apothecaries, London
LMSSA – Licentiate in Medicine and Surgery of the Society of Apothecaries, London
LAH – Licentiate of Apothecaries' Hall, Dublin (Ireland)

Appendix 3

ALPHABETICAL LIST OF
USEFUL CONTACTS

Access to Archives (A2A) – database of archives held in England and Wales
Website: www.a2a.org.uk

AIM25 – Archives in London and the M25 area.
Website: www.aim25.ac.uk

Anaesthesia Heritage Centre
Association of Anaesthetists of Great Britain and Ireland, 21 Portland Place,
London W1B 1PY
Tel: 020 7631 1650
Email: heritage@aagbi.org
Website: http://aagbi.org/heritage/heritagecentre.htm

Apothecaries Hall of Ireland
95 Merrion Square, Dublin, County Dublin 2, Republic of Ireland
Tel: +353 (0) 1 762 147

Archon Directory – information on record repositories in Britain
Website: www.nationalarchives.gov.uk/archon

Army Medical Services Museum
Keogh Barracks, Ash Vale, Aldershot GU12 5RQ
Tel: 01252 868 612
Email: armymedicalmuseum@btinternet.com
Website: www.ams-museum.org.uk

Army Personnel Centre
APC MS Support – Disclosures 4, MP 555, Kentigern House, 65 Brown Street,
Glasgow G2 8EX
Tel: 0845 600 9663
Email: disc4@apc.army.mod.uk
Website: www.army.mod.uk/welfare-support/family/6980.aspx

British Dental Association Museum
64 Wimpole Street, London W1G 8YS
Tel: 020 7935 0875
Email: museum@bda.org
Website: www.bda.org/museum

The British Library (newspapers)
Newspapers, Colindale Avenue, London NW9 5HE
Tel: 020 7412 7353
Email: newspaper@bl.uk
Website: www.bl.uk

The British Library (general enquiries)
St Pancras, 96 Euston Road, London NW1 2DB
Tel: 020 7412 7676
Email: reader-services-enquiries@bl.uk
Website: www.bl.uk

British Nurses' & Hospital Badge Society (BNHBS)
58 Haydons Road, Wimbledon, London SW19 1HL
Tel: 020 8543 9514
Email: bnhbsarchive@hotmail.com
Website: www.bnhbs.freeservers.com

British Optical Association Museum
The College of Optometrists, 42 Craven Street, London WC2N 5NG
Tel: 020 7766 4353
Email: museum@college-optometrists.org
Website: www.college-optometrists.org

British Red Cross Museum and Archives
44 Moorfields, London EC2Y 9AL
Tel: 020 7877 7058
Email: enquiry@redcross.org.uk
Website: www.redcross.org.uk

The Chartered Society of Physiotherapy
14 Bedford Row, London WC1R 4ED
Tel: 020 7306 6666
Website: www.csp.org.uk

Commonwealth War Graves Commission
2 Marlow Road, Maidenhead, Berkshire SL6 7DX
Tel: 01628 634221
Website: www.cwgc.org

Dumfries and Galloway Health Board Archives
Easterbrook Hall, Crichton Royal Hospital, Bankend Road, Dumfries
DG1 4TG
Tel: 01387 244 228

Florence Nightingale Museum
2 Gassiot House, Lambeth Palace Road, London SE1 7EW
Tel: 020 7620 0374
Email: info@florence-nightingale.co.uk
Website: www.florence-nightingale.co.uk

General Register Office
Certificate Services Section, PO Box 2, Southport PR8 2JD
Tel: 0845 603 7788
Email: certificate.services@ips.gsi.gov.uk
Website: www.gro.gov.uk/gro/content/certificates

George Marshall Medical Museum
Charles Hastings Education Centre, Worcestershire Royal Hospital, Worcester
WR5 1DD
Tel: 01905 760 738
Email: catriona.smellie@worcsacute.nhs.uk
Website: www.medicalmuseum.org.uk

Guildhall Library
Aldermanbury, London EC2P 2EJ
Tel: 020 7332 1868
Email: guildhall.library@cityoflondon.gov.uk
Website: www.cityoflondon.gov.uk

Highland Health Board Archives
University of Stirling, Highland Campus, Old Perth Road, Inverness IV2 3JH
Tel: 01463 255607
Email: rp5@stir.ac.uk
Website: www.is.stir.ac.uk/libraries/collections/highlandspeccoll.php

Hospital Records Database – information on location of UK hospital records
Website: www.nationalarchives.gov.uk/hospitalrecords

Imperial War Museum
Lambeth Road, London SE1 6HZ
Tel: 020 7416 5320
Email: mail@iwm.rg.uk
Website: www.iwm.org.uk

International Committee of the Red Cross
Archives Division and Research Service, 19 Avenue de la Paix, Geneva CH-1202, Switzerland
Email: archives.gva@icrc.org
Website: www.icrc.org

King's College London Archives Services
Information Services and Systems, King's College London, Strand, London WC2R 2LS
Tel: 020 7848 2015
Email: archives@kcl.ac.uk
Website: www.kcl.ac.uk/archives

Lambeth Palace Library
Lambeth Palace Road, London SE1 7JU
Tel: 020 7898 1400
Email: lpl.staff@c-of-e.org.uk
Website: www.lambethpalacelibrary.org

London Metropolitan Archives
40 Northampton Road, Clerkenwell, London EC1R 0HB
Tel: 020 7332 3820
Email: ask.lma@cityoflondon.gov.uk
Website: www.lma.gov.uk

London Museums of Health & Medicine – portal for London medical museums
Website: www.medicalmuseums.org/family-history

London Probate Registry
First Avenue House, 42–49 High Holborn, London WC1V 6NP
Tel: 020 7947 6939
Email: londonpersonalapplicationsenquiries@hmcourts-service.gsi.gov.uk
Website: www.hmcourts-service.gov.uk/HMCSCourtFinder/Search.do

Lothian Health Services Archive
Edinburgh University Library, George Square, Edinburgh EH8 9LJ
Tel: 0131 650 3392
Email: lhsa@ed.ac.uk
www.lhsa.lib.ed.ac.uk

The Mitchell Library
North Street, Glasgow G3 7DN
Tel: 0141 287 2999
Email: archives@csglasgow.org
Website: www.mitchelllibrary.org

The National Archives
Ruskin Avenue, Kew, Richmond, Surrey TW9 4DU
Tel: 020 8876 3444
Email: enquiry@nationalarchives.gov.uk
Website: www.nationalarchives.gov.uk

The National Archives of Ireland
Bishop Street, Dublin 8, Ireland
Tel: + 353 (0)1 407 2300
Email: mail@nationalarchives.ie
Website: www.nationalarchives.ie

The National Archives of Scotland
H M General Register House, 2 Princes Street, Edinburgh EH1 3YY
Tel: 0131 535 1314
Email: enquiries@nas.gov.uk
Website: www.nas.gov.uk

National Army Museum
Royal Hospital Road, Chelsea, London SW3 4HT
Tel: 020 7730 0717
Email: info@national-army-museum.ac.uk
Website: www.national-army-museum.ac.uk

NHS Greater Glasgow and Clyde Board Archive
Glasgow University Archives and Business Centre, 77–87 Dumbarton Road,
Glasgow G11 6PW (postal address only)
Tel: 0141 330 2992
Email: a.tough@archives.gla.ac.uk
www.archives.gla.ac.uk/gghb

Northern Health Services Archives
Victoria Pavilion, Aberdeen Royal Infirmary, Woolmanhill, Aberdeen
AB25 1LD
Tel: 01224 555562
Email: f.watson@nhs.net
www.nhsgrampian.org

The Old Operating Theatre & Herb Garret
9a St Thomas St, London SE1 9RY
Tel: 020 7188 2679
Email: curator@thegarret.org.uk
Website: www.thegarret.org.uk

Order of St John Library and Museum
St John's Gate, Clerkenwell, London EC1M 4DA
Tel: 020 7324 4070
Email: museum@nhq.sja.org.uk
Website: www.sja.org.uk/museum

Queen Alexandra's Royal Army Nursing Corps Museum
Keogh Barracks, Ash Vale, Aldershot GU12 5RQ
Tel: 01252 340212
Email: armymedicalmuseum@btinternet.com
Website: www.ams-museum.org.uk/historyQARANC.htm

The Queen's Nursing Institute
3 Albemarle Way, London EC1V 4RQ
Tel: 020 7549 1400
Website: www.qni.org.uk

RAF Personnel Records
RAF Disclosures, Room 221b, Trenchard Hall, RAF Cranwell, Sleaford, Lincs
NG34 8HB
Website: www.raf.mod.uk/links/contacts.cfm

Royal British Nurses Association
The Princess Royal House, The Territorial Army Centre, London Road,
Stonecot Hill, Sutton, Surrey SM3 9HG
Tel: 020 8335 3691
Email: enquiries@rbna.org.uk
Website: www.r-bna.com

The Royal College of Midwives
15 Mansfield Street, London W1G 9NH
Tel: 020 7312 3535
Email: info@rcm.org.uk
Website: www.rcm.org.uk

Royal College of Nursing Archives
42 South Oswald Road, Edinburgh EH9 2HH
Tel: 0131 662 6122
Email: archives@rcn.org.uk
Website: www.rcn.org.uk/development/rcn_archives

Royal College of Obstetricians and Gynaecologists
Information Services, 27 Sussex Place, Regent's Park, London NW1 4RG
Tel: 0207 772 6277
Email: archives@rcog.org.uk
Website: www.rcog.org.uk

Royal College of Physicians of Edinburgh
9 Queen Street, Edinburgh EH2 1JQ
Tel: 0131 225 7324
Email: library@rcpe.ac.uk
Website: www.rcpe.ac.uk

Royal College of Physicians of London
11 St Andrews Place, Regent's Park, London NW1 4LE
Tel: 020 3075 1543
Email: heritage@rcplondon.ac.uk
Website: www.rcplondon.ac.uk/history-heritage/Pages/history-heritage.aspx

Royal College of Physicians and Surgeons of Glasgow
232–42 St Vincent Street, Glasgow G2 5RJ
Tel: 0141 221 6072
Email: library@rcpsg.ac.uk
Website: www.rcpsg.ac.uk

Royal College of Physicians of Ireland
6 Kildare Street, Dublin 2
Tel: +353 (0)1 863 9700
Email: info@numbersix.ie
Website: www.rcpi.ie

The Royal College of Psychiatrists
17 Belgrave Square, London SW1X 8PG
Tel: 020 7235 2351
Website: www.rcpsych.ac.uk

The Royal College of Surgeons of Edinburgh
Library and Archive, Nicolson Street, Edinburgh EH8 9DW
Tel: 0131 527 1630
Email: library@rcsed.ac.uk
Website: www.rcsed.ac.uk

Royal College of Surgeons of England
35–43 Lincoln's Inn Fields, London WC2A 3PE
Tel: 020 7869 6555
Email: library@rcseng.ac.uk
Website: www.rcseng.ac.uk

Royal Pharmaceutical Society of Great Britain Museum
1 Lambeth High Street, London SE1 7JN
Tel: 020 7572 2210
Email: museum@rpsgb.org
Website: www.rpsgb.org/museum

St Bartholomew's Museum and Archives
North Wing, St Bartholomew's Hospital, West Smithfield, London EC1A 7BE
Tel: 020 7601 8152
Email: barts.archives@bartsandthelondon.nhs.uk
Website: www.bartsandthelondon.nhs.uk/aboutus

Scottish Archive Network (SCAN) – database of archives held in Scotland
Website: www.scan.org.uk

Service Personnel and Veterans Agency (SPVA)
MOD Medal Office, Building 250, Imjin Barracks, RAF Innsworth, Gloucester
GL3 1HW
Tel: 0141 224 3600 (MOD Medal enquiry line)
Email: JPAC@spva.mod.uk
Website: www.mod/uk/DefenceInternet/DefenceFor/Veterans/Medals/

The Society of Genealogists
14 Charterhouse Buildings, Goswell Road, London EC1M 7BA
Tel: 020 7251 8799
Email: genealogy@sog.org.uk
Website: www.sog.org.uk

The Society of Radiographers
207 Providence Square, Mill Street, London SE1 2EW
Tel: 020 7740 7200
Website: www.sor.org

Tayside Health Board Archive
Archive Services, University of Dundee, Dundee DD1 4HN
Tel: 01382 384 095
Email: archives@dundee.ac.uk
Website: www.dundee.ac.uk/archives

Tayside Medical History Museum
Ninewells Hospital, Dundee DD1 9SY
Tel: 01382 384310
Email: museum@dundee.ac.uk
Website: www.dundee.ac.uk/museum/medical.htm

Thackray Museum
Beckett Street, Leeds LS9 7LN
Tel: 0113 244 4343
Email: info@thackraymuseum.org
Website: www.thackraymuseum.org

Wellcome Collection
183 Euston Road, London NW1 2BE
Tel: 020 7611 2222
Email: info@wellcomecollection.org
Website: www.wellcomecollection.org

Wellcome Library
183 Euston Road, London NW1 2BE
Tel: 020 7611 8722
Email: library@wellcome.ac.uk
Website: http://library.wellcome.ac.uk/index.html

Women's Transport Service (FANY)
TA Centre, 95 Horseferry Road, London SW1P 2DX
Tel: 020 7976 5459
Email: hq@fany.org.uk
Website: www.fany.org.uk

The Worshipful Society of Apothecaries of London
Apothecaries Hall, Black Friars Lane, London EC4V 6EJ
Tel: 020 7248 6648
Email: archivist@apothecaries.org
Website: www.apothecaries.org

York Probate Sub-Registry
First Floor, Castle Chambers, Clifford Street, York YO1 7EA
Tel: 01904 666 777
Email: YorkPSRenquiries@hmcourts-service.gsi.gov.uk
Website: www.hmcourts-service.gov.uk/HMCSCourtFinder/CourtList.do

Appendix 4
BIBLIOGRAPHY

Abel-Smith, Brian, *The Hospitals, 1800–1948: A Study in Social Administration in England and Wales* (Heinemann, 1964)

Baly, Monica E, 'The Nightingale Nurses: The Myth and the Reality', in Maggs, Christopher (ed.), *Nursing History: The State of the Art* (Croom Helm, 1987), pp. 33–59

Barclay, Jean, *In Good Hands: The History of the Chartered Society of Physiotherapy 1894–1994* (Butterworth Heinemann, 1994)

Berridge, Virginia, 'Health and Medicine', in Thompson, F M L (ed.), *The Cambridge Social History of Britain 1750–1950, Volume 3: Social Agencies and Institutions* (Cambridge University Press, 1993)

Black, Nick, *Walking London's Medical History* (The Royal Society of Medicine Press Limited, 2006)

Blaker, Nathaniel Paine, *Sussex in Bygone Days: Reminiscences of Nathaniel Paine Blaker, MRCS* (N P Blaker, 1919)

Booth, Charles, *Life and Labour of the People in London* (Williams and Norgate, 1891)

Bourne, Susan and Chicken, Andrew H, *Records of the Medical Professions: A Practical Guide for the Family Historian* (S Bourne and A H Chicken, 1994)

Boyd, Julia, *The Excellent Doctor Blackwell: The Life of the First Woman Physician* (Sutton Publishing, 2005)

Brittain, Vera, *Testament of Youth* (Virago Press Limited, 1978)

Brown, G H, *Lives of the Fellows of the Royal College of Physicians of London, Volume 4, 1826–1925* (Royal College of Physicians, 1955)

Bynum, W F, *Science and the Practice of Medicine in the Nineteenth Century* (Cambridge University Press, 1994)

Chamberlain, Geoffrey, *From Witchcraft to Wisdom: A History of Obstetrics and Gynaecology in the British Isles* (RCOG Press, 2007)

Cherry, Steven, *Medical Services and the Hospitals in Britain 1860–1939* (Cambridge University Press, 1996)

Clark-Kennedy, A E, *The London: A Study in the Voluntary Hospital System* (Pitman Medical Publishing Company, 1963)

Delpratt Harris, J, *The Royal Devon and Exeter Hospital* (Eland Bros, 1922)

Dingwall, Robert, Rafferty, Anne Marie and Webster, Charles, *An Introduction to the Social History of Nursing* (Routledge, 1988)

Halliday, Stephen, *The Great Filth: The War Against Disease in Victorian England* (Sutton Publishing, 2007)

Hamilton, David, *The Healers: A History of Medicine in Scotland* (Canongate, 1981)

Hardy, Anne, *Health and Medicine in Britain Since 1860* (Palgrave Macmillan, 2001)

Higgs, Michelle, *Life in the Victorian Hospital* (The History Press, 2009)

Hillam, Christine, *Brass Plate and Brazen Impudence: Dental Practice in the Provinces 1755–1855* (Liverpool University Press, 1991)

Holloway, S W F, *Royal Pharmaceutical Society of Great Britain 1841–1991: A Political and Social History* (The Pharmaceutical Press, 1991)

Howse, Carrie, *Rural District Nursing in Gloucestershire 1880–1925* (Reardon Publishing, 2008)

Jack, T C and Jack, E C, *Jack's Reference Book* (T. C. & E. C. Jack Ltd., 1916)

Lane, Joan, *John Hall and his Patients: The Medical Practice of Shakespeare's Son-in-Law* (Sutton Publishing, 1996)

Lane, Joan, *A Social History of Medicine: Health, Healing and Disease in England, 1750–1950* (Routledge, 2001)

Loudon, Irvine, *Medical Care and the General Practitioner 1750–1850* (Clarendon Press, 1986)

Lückes, Eva, *Lectures on General Nursing* (Kegan Paul, Trench & Co., 1884)

Maggs, Christopher (ed.), *Nursing History: The State of the Art* (Croom Helm, 1987)

Matthews, L G, *The History of Pharmacy in Britain* (Livingstone Limited, 1962)

Mitchell, Margaret, *History of the British Optical Association 1895–1978* (The British Optical Association, 1982)

Munk, William, *Roll of the Royal College of Physicians of London, Volumes 1 and 2, 1518–1800* (Longman, Green, Longman and Roberts, 1861)

Munk, William, *Roll of the Royal College of Physicians of London, Volume 3, 1801–1825* (Royal College of Physicians, 1861)

Peel, Sir John, *The Lives of the Fellows of the Royal College of Obstetricians and Gynaecologists 1929–1969* (Heinemann Medical Books, 1976)

Pelling, Margaret, *The Common Lot: Sickness, Medical Occupations and the Urban Poor in Early Modern England* (Longman, 1998)

Peterkin, A, Johnston, W and Drew, R, *Commissioned Officers in the Medical Services of the British Army* (Wellcome Historical Medical Library, 1968)

Plarr, Victor and Power, Sir D'Arcy (eds), *Plarr's Lives of the Fellows of the Royal College of Surgeons of England, Volumes 1 and 2, 1843–1929* (J Wright & Sons Ltd, 1930)

Porter, Roy, *Blood & Guts: A Short History of Medicine* (Penguin Books, 2002)

Porter, Roy (ed.), *The Cambridge Illustrated History of Medicine* (Cambridge University Press, 2001)

Power, Sir D'Arcy and Le Fanu, W R, *Lives of the Fellows of the Royal College of Surgeons of England, Volume 3, 1930–1951* (Royal College of Surgeons of England, 1953)

Royston Pike, E, *Human Documents of the Age of the Forsytes* (George Allen and Unwin, 1969)

Shorter, Edward, 'Primary Care', in Porter, Roy (ed.), *The Cambridge Illustrated History of Medicine* (Cambridge University Press, 2001)

Stevenson, John, *British Society 1914–1945* (Penguin Books, 1984)

Summers, Anne, *Angels and Citizens: British Women as Military Nurses 1854–1914* (Threshold Press, 2000)

Sykes, Keith with Bunker, John, *Anaesthesia and the Practice of Medicine: Historical Perspectives* (The Royal Society of Medicine Press Limited, 2007)

Thompson, F M L (ed.), *The Cambridge Social History of Britain 1750–1950, Volume 3, Social Agencies and Institutions* (Cambridge University Press, 1993)

Trail, Richard Robertson, *Lives of the Fellows of the Royal College of Physicians of London, Volume 4, 1926–1965* (Royal College of Physicians, 1965)

Waddy, F F, *A History of Northampton General Hospital 1743 to 1948* (The Guildhall Press (Northampton) Limited, 1974)

Articles in periodicals

Burnby, Juanita G L, 'A Study of the English Apothecary from 1660 to 1760', *Medical History*, Supplement No. 3, 1983

Crellin, J K, 'Pharmaceutical History and its Sources in the Wellcome Collections: The Growth of Professionalism in Nineteenth Century British Pharmacy', *Medical History*, July 1967

Halliday, Stephen, 'Delivering the Goods', *BBC Who Do You Think You Are?* , December 2007

Mansford, Augusta E, 'Hospital Days and Hospital Ways', *The Strand Magazine*, January 1895

McKenzie, Fred A, 'The London Hospital', *The Windsor Magazine*, XIII, 49, December 1900

'Nurses of Note – Mrs Rebecca Strong', *British Journal of Nursing*, January 1924

Royall, Arthur, 'Eva Lückes: Too Young and Too Pretty', *Family Tree*, October 2007

Wrench, Edward M, 'The Lessons of the Crimean War', *British Medical Journal*, 22 July 1899

Periodicals and newspapers

British Journal of Nursing
British Medical Journal
The Graphic
Illustrated London News
Lancet
Nursing Record
Provincial Medical Journal
The Strand Magazine
The Times
The Windsor Magazine

Websites

HHARP (Historic Hospital Admission Registers Project): www.hharp.org (Kingston University)

Higginbotham, Peter: The Workhouse www.workhouses.org.uk

Jackson, Lee: The Victorian Dictionary www.victorianlondon.org

Rivett, G C: National Health Service History www.nhshistory.net

INDEX